INSPIRATION ABOUT LIFE OR LOVE

By
MALVIN SIBUSISO TSHABANGU

TIE PUBLISHER

*Love is Deep
and the
Masters
of
Life*

First published by Tie Publisher 2022

Copyright © 2022 by Tshabangu Sibusiso Malvin

All rights reserved. No part of this publication may be reproduced, stored or transmitted in any form or by any means, electronic, mechanical, photocopying, recording, scanning, or otherwise without written permission from the publisher. It is illegal to copy this book, post it to a website, or distribute it by any other means without permission.

This novel is entirely a work of fiction. The names, characters and incidents portrayed in it are the work of the author's imagination. Any resemblance to actual persons, living or dead, events or localities is entirely coincidental.

Sibusiso Tshabangu asserts the moral right to be identified as the author of this work.

Sibusiso Tshabangu has no responsibility for the persistence or accuracy of URLs for external or third-party Internet Websites referred to in this publication and does not guarantee that any content on such Websites is, or will remain, accurate or appropriate.

Designations used by companies to distinguish their products are often claimed as trademarks. All brand names and product names used in this book and on its cover are trade names, service marks, trademarks and registered trademarks of their respective owners. The publishers and the book are not associated with any product or vendor mentioned in this book. None of the companies referenced within the book have endorsed the book.

First edition

ISBN: 978-0-6397-2101-9

This book was professionally typeset by

Tie Publisher

Thank you for the support, in everything that I've been doing, that has provided the knowledge to write this book; for the character you've resembled, it took a long time to reach a conclusion that creates a simple and understandable solution, that we all can be able to relate to, no matter who you are and where you from.

No matter who you are or where you come from, a complete understanding about life and true love is our gift to perfection and happiness.

Table of Contents

Foreword I
Preface VIII
Acknowledgements X
Twenty four seven 2
Lean on love 11
Virtues of love 19
Elements of love 27
Slice of life 36
Love Intuition 46
The exchange of life 56
Passion 66
Center of life 76
Flow of life 85
True love 93
Spark of Love 108
Love Drops 118
Love is deep 128
Island in the Sea 138
Test of Life 148
Gift of Life 159
Measure of Love 168
Masters of Life 179
A Way of Life 191
Quality of the Heart 202

Foreword

From the depth of our soul, we find ourselves stuck and lost in situations of life, about love and how so much could have been if I had never met this person. Who at one point could have been the best thing that has ever happened to me, it becomes part of the most amazing feeling anyone has ever had to share with someone. Especially when is truly connecting you, from deep inside, and you give everything that you have for each other without holding anything back.

It is the moments that we share that can be unforgettable, leading to an act of life's most romantic journeys we have ever taken into each other's hearts. Uncovering and exploring the most hidden and sacred places within our bodies, discovering the beauty about our existence. The tenderness that is reflected by the softness of our skins, love, and of who we are. Something we don't quite often exchange with anyone, but with the only one we surrender our hearts to, and if you don't know how to give and treasure that, you are likely to spend the rest of your livelihood alone.

We sacrifice a lot just to resemble how much we love and care for each other, taking that extra mile to be with the only one that your heart longs for. The trouble that relationships can put you through as a reflection of growth and determination in loving one another. Then the reality of what we always know about communions comes, arguments, fights, separation, and then the emotional effect that commitment can have on anyone who has ever loved truly.

How miserable someone can become without the other, that had formed part of who you are, which we know represents a lot of people that we see daily being lost from their past affections.

One can lose interest on everything good about our lives; the loss of someone whom you have cared for deeply can have a huge impact on who you become in the future. Just to have that special person cut off your life without being prepared for anything, you can suffer a huge emotional setback. Having to learn how to be on your own, even if you manage to move forward by yourself, you don't forget easily that you once loved.

You cannot always find the right person, people differ spiritually and physically, through contact and sharing feelings deeply, you become aware of new experiences in loving a human being. Love doesn't happen every day, and is always that part of life, that you know you were once happy loving someone and you can hardly find that kind of individual ever again.

It takes a lot to build a person's understanding, and when one becomes formed in love, from loving someone, the structure of that human being created by commitment changes. You can become very strong knowing that you have that special being to rely on, when you find yourself destructed from that, through life's unforeseen experiences. Then the mind becomes very ill, it weakens, spiritually you cannot advance forward clearly. The battle you have to face, whereas the destruction can be permanent, in other circumstances you can have this huge or mental effect just to move on with everything normally.

The psychological effect known for being committed and ending up separated can be very destructive in nature. Yet if you cherish the idea of remaining trustworthy to the same person that you have always been with, you become a very productive individual. A lot of people have become strong and influential early in life loving the same person every day, Confidence comes from knowing that you love someone who relies on you and you rely on them.

It is changing along the way that can make one feel very disturbed just to go on with life normally. Part of which can also apply to your well-being as well, to truly find happiness you must build reliability on your goals, refused to be influenced by circumstances.

Being normally involved with love truly, will once again depend on the level of discipline that one has, so much about who we are is that we don't call ourselves back to focus. In some way we become obsessed with believing on the fact that, being separated from our loved ones can be healed by certain aspects of life, other than true love.

Sometimes it calls on discipline, that if you know how to be truly disciplined, then you learn how to follow your heart. Forget about so much that has happened and other people along the way, be true to your inner self, and only focus on that face of life and love the best way you know how.

The option becomes the one that you have chosen for yourself, you can either choose to be happy or you can spend years, months, and days lost in affection. When you lose self-discipline, love just comes to catch up with you once in a while. You owe it to life, to be focused, given that without good morals, you can never be too sure about how you want things to be.

Lean on love, we know that we are never guilty of anything there is, still something keeps on fighting with us. Only that we choose our ways, you can always settle for anything, or you can strive to find true love, as we are all affected by the modernization of things, and the rapid change of the world. The universe has moved on faster than we have ever expected, and that has had a major impact on how we feel about one another.

Life took a turn into modernization, relationships and things are not what they use to be, because human beings have studied and experimented beyond limits, about everything that they know, and understand. Whether we get it right or not we always come back to that sense of passion and loving one another. Whatever people experiment with, could eventually come into light, through the act of intimacy without anyone understanding how our lives and love could have influence the subjects of science, and how that could later have a major impact on human beings.

All that we have seen is people's discoveries, and what we didn't see is their disappointments or where they've failed, love is strong, it can be able to manifest all that a person has been thinking or doing. However in today's world we want to understand how we became a mark of ignorance, why do we overlook our partners, why look away from such a beautiful part of ourselves, and fail to ever find who we are again?

Why can't life be easy for one to just make a worthless decision and comes back to rectify it? That's because the world has changed and there are no more rooms for mistakes, when it comes to relationships, personal goals, and loving one another, a lot of important things has now become the target for everyone.

Man and women must gear up and begin to consider love, relationships, and family very seriously, as you might not get a second chance to find happiness, even if you ever get that opportunity it won't come easy. Today we must fear what human beings have tried and get right, only to become influential in people's lives, and not in all areas of life.

So much is not said about who we are, only what we were able to manifest, has been taken into account, the rest doesn't matter, but that doesn't mean it won't be able to affect people out there, we can become subject of everything that human beings have created in the world.

Once you come across their creations, you are not only taken away where you needed to know, you have been disturbed all over your understanding, where you work, love, or even where you are a human being. So much is involved in what people do, they teach a lot about this world and our lives, is just how we are trying to make a living out of this beautiful planet. Yet little teaches about relationships and understands how that can be important not only in your life, also in the well-being of those who you inspire and influence very much.

With all the rapid change, innovation, and technological trends that there are today, human beings must be very cautious, so one thing is to be careful and not to ever lose focus on what matters the most. Regardless of who you are, a lot that you come across, can harm you, or take away something vital in you; and that's the reason our relationships must always be protected by our hearts, knowledge, and higher understanding.

Do not allow anything to destruct you, towards focusing on your heart's felt passion or love, it must be allowed a space to rule from deep within, and strive to protect it with our whole life. Give everything that you have, so that you mustn't be disturbed by whatever comes your way and regret the chances you had to live for true love.

The thing is that you can make a mistake and rectify it, right now before it ruins that much, so what if someone, once in a lifetime fails to undo their errors and get taken away entirely? You look at yourself and where you are, only to find that you have disappeared permanently, and no matter what you do, you can never find who you were again.

It happens all the time that you are, what you understand best, and no matter what the frustrations of the day can do to try and change your life, you would remain the same, and you ask yourself, what am I holding on to? You leaning on love and loving your partner, the essence of your values in sharing what you are with that special person, you have found your purpose. No matter what situations can throw towards your direction, you wouldn't allow to be turned into something that you not. As you know where you headed, regardless of what someone might convince you to become.

We are never certain if all of the world's most important concepts apply to whether you know what you doing or not, yet there's one thing for sure. That the love you have in your heart is enough, like it is, that you can never be driven in a similar path all of you. Some can find who they are right now, others later, while someone can never at all understands what is it that they had been doing, life taken for good.

Only if you strong enough loving a human being, that all these lives will come to pass and nothing can ever stay there forever, that's how you can remain focus in everything that you care for. If you're ever lost from lack of devotion and affection, you may try to find closure, yet there's no one around you. These life's work can take you away from yourself and isolate you, and if true love isn't there, you are not being groomed where you are important to your well-being.

You are highly valued where you have loved, that's how priceless you are to everything that there is. Even when you approach something you can only find satisfaction in two ways, love or money, either one of the two will make you happy. Whether I know what I'm doing or not, I always expect to earn something in return and be tucked in someone's arms.

I am selling things into a world that cannot afford what I'm doing, what do I take in return? Love, so what if we have the means to acquire what you have to offer? Then take your money, it is always necessary, that you must be careful when it comes to matters of the heart, don't give away something, which you can never have back.

Always remember before you live your home, that your family is the most important part of your life. All that follows after you have left your house, or which you brought back with you, amounts to nothing compared to what you have already.

The time you have had with the ones you love is not to be compromised for anything, just because I don't like or enjoy the same hobbies with you, it doesn't mean we have nothing in common. We can have so many separate views, it all doesn't matter, everything comes after we have loved each other completely, and we can have one mutual opinion, of the true love that has brought us together. The value of a human being that you have been with every day cannot be overlooked for anyone or anything.

It's all wrongdoing or too wrong to overlook a person that you have been with so deeply, our hearts should be able to find a home in the other, and it must be stable. Even though it is where we coming from, where we had to look out for ourselves in terms of love and loving one another. That it is no longer a threat to give yourself to someone, and that a human being cannot be deceived by anything or anyone, and we had been left to our own mistakes. That if we ever make that error of not committing to each other truly, then it happened accidentally and no one should account for it.

Now that we have reached a certain stage, where you can see that some things are made by human beings just for them to get the better out of life, it was always good when no one would want to benefit from that. So given the circumstances that people have realized all these opportunities out there, and have begun taking advantage of the situation, and they are now capitalizing on our mistakes.

Love was never a threat or taken into consideration as something that needed protection, but it now represents one of the loopholes whereby everything can creep into your life. You can find human beings that were knocked out from true love that no longer exist in the reality that we live in today.

Things changed and they never became effective, whereas they form part of the active generation that we have today, and they will cost us so much and our lives as well. How do you bring someone like that back to reality, when the universe fights so hard just to defy a human being? If a certain world takes you out of circulation it will fight you with everything that exists not to ever become a valid person again.

No matter what you try it could become impossible to ever come back to reality, and you have been consumed where you matter to yourself. You can linger there forever, lord knows, when you will ever be able to understand how to break free, these are some of the most important things that you must be aware of. Highly dangerous world of human beings who exists only to devour love and so much more, and they came into your heart through lacking care when it comes to committing to that special person.

So remember all the time to love your partner more, show gratitude and commit deeper every day to that unique individual who allowed you into their lives. So that you can never be lost again, on anything or any occasion, not many can understand how to bring a human being back. Yet for now those who can't help themselves, maybe through realizing how important commitment is. They can be pulled from within the center of life, and made to acknowledge that true love is worth being cherished.

You don't need to have anything before you can realize how important your partner is, people have zero tolerance for mistakes in relationships.

Preface

Love as one of the most essential subjects in our lives, became an inspiration for me to reflect on, because of how so much has changed in this modern society, and how we should devote our whole lives to loving our partners in our relationships every day. How imperative it is to give true commitment to someone who loves you; and how you must understand that your life depends on being honest to your partner to be productive in all areas. As that kind of union is one of the most precious gifts you can ever give to each other.

So much that we are is mostly influenced by how we respond to each other, the minute you lose someone that you loved, you start losing focus on the most important parts of your well-being. Relationships and life are dependent on one another for human beings to find the real purpose to what they're living for. Failing to commit to our partners can become part of the weaknesses we have adopted within. You must learn to value the other as everything that there is, can find a gap to come into your lives through love.

A lot that there is around us, are things that have been created and mastered by human beings who gave their lives and love to seeing something coming into being. Although these are some very important and good parts of our daily well-being, if in some other instances you have been found without true love in your heart. So much could be able to creep into your soul in a way that you can never be able to understand your true purpose.

The world has advanced further and faster than man and woman have ever anticipated, if you lose focus on love. You can become a victim of situations and circumstances of these new societies and other forms of modernization the world has become today. Part of which could be difficult to ever find yourself where everything was once true in your life.

So much has been mastered in a way that, there is nothing of this world remaining, now love has turned to be the target in everything, because that's the essence of creation. With all that is happening around us, relationships have become the shelter for human beings to hide from whatever is going on within our environment. The universe has changed somewhere so deep and there are no more rooms for mistakes. The way we people can be ignorant of loving each other completely, has resulted in so many opting for anything available.

Is not like true love doesn't exist, it does, from the moment you decide to fall in love with someone. You must be able to understand that your life has begun accounting for everything that you will be doing within that relationship. You need to live well knowing that you consider your partner, don't misuse any chance you get to be with your loved one. Make sure you take any opportunity available to be with someone and use it wisely to please each other.

We only have few chances to find true love, the universe is always looking at us and everything that we doing. If you in some way lack appreciation for someone's presence, so much can disappoint you, because you can never be sure whom you will fall in love with in the next turn. Life can only offer us little opportunities for true commitment, after that has disappeared, reality disappears where it used to be what we know. You now become subject to what has been created and mastered by other human beings, and that can fail you a lot as it is where the world is no longer real.

Acknowledgements

My greatest acknowledgments and gratitude to all who have provided the platform and love for making and reading books possible.

Thank you!!!

Part One

Twenty four seven

You take a walk searching for something, which matters the most to a human being on a daily basis, and all that you find are matters of life and conflict in relationships. What really complicates our lives and love at the center of humanity, what restrains so many from finding true happiness?

There are ways to begin understanding, what could interrupt the flow of life and love between human beings, there are so many reasons to why and what. However, to tell the truth, my understanding has been moving closer to the center, to get clarity about the reality we live in, and what could go wrong in a relationship and why you have to honestly reflect from deep within. To help you reconnect with yourself again.

I took a reflection towards studying a certain aspect of love we call the masters of life, my understanding on how we view reality begins here. I try to find the relationship and meaning of things and how one can tackle this kind of issues if you understand or motivated enough.

Love at times, from my perspective seemed to have no solution, and you cannot put the blame on human beings that have transcended beyond the ordinary substances. Sometimes it is our own doing that complicates our lives, the Masters of life focuses on issues that can affect everyone, and what makes things difficult for people not to move forward with ease.

What is it that alters reality for people not to have solutions to finding true love easily? We dwell in a universe filled with issues that we have never known how to solve, and when something goes wrong, you have to reflect on those situations. For those who haven't been pushed into that defying world, then you still live on the safe side of life.

It is part of those things that affects any man or woman, cases of unsolved controversies about love, marriage, our lives, or happiness. These are some of the issues that we refer to, as the masters of life, matters standing before a human being and his destiny. Knowing that we all can get there, now how do you find a path to that place, where your heart truly longs to be.

In today's world, it is not about being single, it is the emotional setback that one can go through, unable to find an easy route. How do you pass through these gates, or to be able to avoid this kind of issues when you still have so much needs? Passing through the cycle of life's difficulties without contracting anything.

Remember that it exists within a certain age that you had your youth, and you can only have that once in a lifetime, and you don't want to miss on an opportunity to have lived. This is where man and woman have become vulnerable to everything out there, through the needs that they have. As you cannot sacrifice your chances of finding happiness at the end of the day.

What human beings require is a solution to specifically point out, here is where things have gone wrong, that drove them apart, and why they need to separate. Love is the only thing that got people, so hard to believe, but has true love ever been practiced or achieved, and if it has been, then why the need to be separated from one another, if you know you can never be happy with someone else again. How can you ever live with the experience of losing that special person you have loved so deeply, or let alone to ever understand what you were in this diverse reality; and whom can you blame for your loss?

I had put the blame on man and woman who have allowed true love to slip away just like that. Human beings are always moving forward with loving each other, and making love, every night and day, somewhere so deep, and you cannot disturb that kind of flow between individuals committed to one another truly. It is something that remains between two people longing for each other endlessly.

There's always something that wants to separate human beings from committing to each other completely. The work of this kind had mostly been to find any existing path towards people who love one another, and interfering with all that they are. Lovers don't want to be interrupted by anything, they only want to think of themselves when they are involved in sharing who they are, hence the odds will always keep it tight not to allow outside interference.

When you want to find someone to give yourself to after you had separated with the one you loved deeply, you find that human beings are continuing with the same flow of life. So just like that, they make it so impossible for anyone to start over whenever you feel like beginning a new chapter of love.

True love has no reason to love a person, it's a right to be human, but if you ever give up on it, life might require a purpose for you to be loved again. You become similar to someone trying to interfere with things that doesn't concern them. And without a valid explanation why you want to be involved with it once more, why do you want to disturb human beings from doing something that you abandoned?

We must learn to value true love every day of our lives, as there are only few opportunities to find happiness, don't look down on loving someone, commit with everything that you have. Carry that undying faith in giving yourself and pleasing that particular person who cherishes your presence, with all that you can, every day and minute of your life.

Another trigger is failing yourself, by not realizing how important your partner is, which on its own could be the reason why a human being can become very defenseless to every situation of love. There could be the issue of ignorance, which could fail one in a relationship, and again lacking appreciation for someone's presence. That is where a lot of things could have found a path to creep into your heart and interfere with your well-being. You don't consider your lover very well when you are with them, you think less of their presence, although so much can drive such a feeling to overlook caring for a person.

I had seen myself living alone, and trying to know things better, or maybe the only way in which they are. I began by mentioning conflict at the center of our lives, and what could steal that tender of life from a human being, and why? Love could have been the point, to have loved something or someone, so great that it couldn't be said enough. Like it had been told, only in that way, to be separated from a person that you have loved so much with everything that you are, and have spent every day together, could have that effect on an individual.

It could've been the reason that moving closer to the center, made me realize I was the one who abandoned love when I was still capable of loving and giving. How do you come back from such an encounter of existence, learning to let go of everything, and focusing on finding that special person. Which could be, another way you can come back to the reality of loving someone, or other ways you can attract human being's back to your life, or cycle of love and make them forgive you for the separation and loneliness.

Love can look away, and so much will come to pass, and you will have to cope with looking at human beings that are committed to each other, living and moving forward with life until you learn how to value someone's presence with all your heart.

There's always a reason why someone leaves the other, whether you're right or wrong, the cause doesn't justify the pain you will feel of being alone. Love could need both of you to pay special attention to everything that you doing, it doesn't matter who it is in the relationship, focus deeply and exercise caring. Everyone that leaves your life takes away something very crucial and that could be the reason you are stuck and single, because you didn't realize how important some things or person could be. Even though you could try to justify why you had to separate with the one you cared about, but that human being cannot be replaced easily.

You knew how to move someone out of your life, and now you want to set the stage up with another person, and treat it like a normal situation of falling in and out of love. Only that it can never happen so easily, at times it can become very difficult and you might need to be very concerned with loving your partner honestly.

Unlike thinking of setting up the stage just like that, it might not be easy to once again find someone that you can love and trust into a relationship with you. Some situations could turn out to be very difficult that you might realize that there is a psychological matter that has now become part of the scene. Which might want you to deal with the issue not only physically, but also spiritually.

When people have separated and love isn't there anymore, what keeps insisting on leaving you out of every good that exists? How does one stops loving the other when so much could go wrong? Why stop caring for someone you have been with every day? Maybe that doesn't matter that much, what matters is how can you become a human being again? Whoever leaves your life, you could have another to love you once more, but can you find a special one to commit to. So how long will it take to develop a fully functional relationship, and who can fill that space in your heart?

I had thought about it, and never really understand what the difference is, between now and then. I had tried my best to find closure, only that things became too much to evaluate. With separation from true love came situations of trying to heal your heart, and coping with life.

When you thought that your world can never be too dead, as you could've at least achieved something, by trying to heal your heart. Now you have no love from anyone no more, it has disappeared, and it has become difficult to find someone who truly loves you. Back then you had never wronged anyone, and moving forward you have that crime of knowing that I had been happy with my past lover, how can I make peace with loving another person again?

It becomes a very confusing situation for someone to understand, how did the world become so strong? At one point you thought that you can easily achieve your share of life and love, whereas you can't. Maybe now or in the meantime you could hold on to loving yourself because with passion focus towards your ambitions you can achieve a good success story on your own, that's at the end of the day. In a sophisticated world, for those who have died at the center of all that gives, can create a new meaning for themselves. A wonder of creativity; from loving who you are, can work very well in reconnecting with all of existence.

As you had your whole life to love someone and you abandoned it, since you never realized how special that time had been. To just walk away from true love like that, how important the time you have spent together, so great that it can never be repeated. We are all subject to good behaviour, if you make a mistake, you will be punished for it.

Besides our attempts of trying to come back through our own knowledge, I still wanted to understand how deep love is, to what depth can we break apart? And when all has happened that left us torn and heartbroken, what is the process of recovering from such a setback? The masters that defines true love; summarizes healing as a stage of complete understanding after one has overlooked loving a human being first.

It could be to gain recognition or moving forward on your own, and later realizes how important committing to your partner is. Then comes back to acknowledge that only in certain areas of life, you would have achieved your purpose, but not entirely. Only when you have reached a level of complete understanding in loving a human being, that healing can occur, then you can move on to loving that special person and be truly happy.

It started with you neglecting your responsibilities to be with someone, then love was deficient, this is something that happened within the days of your life. When you abandoned true love, you became a different person, a human being spiritually, and you can live out there not recognizing the need to be with that caring individual. Yet you must understand that to find happiness, is first learning to belittle yourself back to your partner's care in physical form.

Regardless of how good you are with everything, it always comes back to love. It is within the days that you learn to appreciate a person that you will find someone with a caring heart to be with you truly. You forget about the world where you excel, and focus on that as your ultimate objective.

We live in a world where things can become very difficult when living with no one to love. Being without that unique person takes away something vital in a human being, and that can steal the tenderness of life and acceptance. To be happy you must know the value of love, what it says about you, or resembles towards other people.

I knew the value of what had been stolen within me, my heart was empty, and so much had been taken away, at the end the world couldn't offer anything better. I had chosen my route searching for love, or maybe my journey towards life and everything that I was doing, and the results of that had been truly amazing and very influential. Only that one needs true love to cope with situations, and be able to handle all that comes your way in a good manner, because deep inside your soul is settled.

Love is not what most of us expect it to be, mostly when you're in a relationship with someone. It is so good it feels like it can last forever, and once you lose that kind of human, especially when you have spent more time together, you begin to feel miserable. Something developed while your hearts were united, a bond of some sort, deep within your soul that knows whom to love and how to fulfill their needs perfectly. It is a part of you that became loyal in loving one person, that it is so deeply involved with that unique individual, it won't settle for anything less than that human being you have been with every day.

Once you become separated from that person and try to find someone or if something else exists out there. Then you realize that there is nothing left, everything you had, disappeared with a man or a woman whom you loved truly. Of which you did have it within you when love still cared for you and supported your daily activities, and when you want all that again, only to be disappointed as it has vanished.

Love is no longer there, that's the part about a human being, and you don't see or find the actual value when they are still here. After they have left your life, they leave a space that cannot be filled easily, it belonged to that one person. It will always be a void, nobody can replace that special being in you.

You look only to find that there is nothing left, and love, when you still know and understand what you're doing with regard to it, has so much to offer and give to human beings. When it is young and good, and knows how to defend itself, then you realize that you have passed that stage and there's no more left for you.

Love was once its entity, it was not to be influenced by situations or other human beings, and it was its own guard. Before you fell in the hands of those who have mastered life, people who have changed the origin of things as we have known them. Always remember they can still snatch you, when you have stopped or abandoned loving your partner, individuals who worked hard to master our everyday lives, know how to manipulate true love to pass you.

These are the true masters of life, that take on a journey to understand everything that there is to know about our well-being or relationships. Things that have been created by man and woman which have come to change people's perceptions, and destined to become a permanent part of our everyday existence. It is the discoveries of the new society, that are here to change the world and how we know it, and they will not be leaving our lives forever. At the end we become dependent on this facets of reality, it is what creates the universe that we live in today.

It forms part of everybody's lives, these are things that can disturb human beings into loving each other. Situations always looking for people who could make a mistake, doubt, or question anything in life or love. Who could fail to realize the importance of what they have, once you look aside, you have been distracted permanently. It seeks for you to recognize the time that you have spent with someone night and day, and to know that is not to be overlooked for anything, and that if you ever let go, you can be without forever.

It is ideas that have been created by human beings, which are very influential and capable of creating our daily lives, and if strong enough can continue to create our everyday life. If an idea like that dominates human being's well-being, they have no option except that they have to allow it to become part of their existence.

It could be something created in any form, health, life, or maybe even love, these are some of the things that can be taken away from people. You find yourself forced to understand what creation has become today, and if not you're being left back on everything that the world has to offer. Such ideas can come and change human being's lives by binding them deeper than anything, especially when it comes to finding love and happiness.

These are some kind of issues that you must be on the lookout for, do not forget to practice good morals in relationships. Make sure that nothing can come in between you and loving that special person, if you ever give it a chance by doubting what you have, you disappear into lack. It is love most that becomes vital to take away from human beings, as one of the precious parts where a human being can become vulnerable.

I wondered how one can come back from such a setback, can the world still be created for those who have broken hearts, or have lost their first love to anything in this complex universe? Can people say that true love does exists, and is something that if you can go out there you will surely come across? And that if you have that question about commitment, you will find the answer in everything that make-up today's life?

So much has changed extremely, it is no longer what it used to be, and that has somehow influenced our lives as well. Everything that we see today has been recreated by human beings, in this vast universe where distance can come in between people and separate them. What is there left, because nothing can ever be fixed, the damage that love can have on humanity opens the gap to eternity.

This universe only caters for those who are still strong in loving one another, if you somehow become distracted from being committed to your partner, then your life has been disturbed permanently. Regardless of how so much has advanced, yet love remains the only thing that is real about us, and refuses to be changed. Now that we're here, we can say that we regret what we have lost along the way, but moving ahead we can try to adapt to this new perspective.

Even if it feels as if we settling for less, maybe we can make it life because true love is gone, and disappeared, now we're only left with this world made from man's understanding. And the fear to go beyond the ordinary substances and discover new love that cannot be changed but can lead us to true commitment, that you can find deep within your soul, and in your heart.

Chapter One

Lean on love

We don't know how much is involved in loving one another. The main theme about love, is to try and understand the level of involvement towards committing to each other, and why do we have to go through breakups, which we can never heal from? Why does one stop caring for someone, you've spent every day with, and worse is how they have put their whole trust on you?

Where do you find the courage of letting go of everything that we've had over the years, how does a woman find the strength to cheat on a man that she had loved forever? And when does a man find the motive to divorce a woman? After all these years, the time we have spent together, the lovemaking, the intimacy that we've shared, and you just let it go, all of it, you give it all away, like that.

This is someone you have spent the rest of your life with, sharing the same bed every day, the first person you see when you wake up. The making of love, the kisses, and the hugs that you exchange on a daily basis, or maybe sharing more than just romance, kids as well. Do we stop caring or love can never fade away unless someone has wronged us, does it matter who is wrong for one to forgive? Who stops believing in the other, and our own creation of mutual respect, of a communion of hearts that were beating for one another?

In our acts, before we act on anything, do we think about the future first? Or we just do it, like that. We look away, and say, it doesn't matter what tomorrow holds, nothing can ever be worse than having to put up with this person, who has brought shame into my life?

Is better to be single than to keep up with this embarrassment that you have become, you shut the door and walk away. Just like that, forever, no regrets, or looking back, you're through, and tomorrow you wake up alone? Who loses hope on loving the other or stops relying on the love that has created a huge family for belonging? Knowing very well, in your heart that a commitment is not for one, is for both of us, when you refuse to have faith in your relationship, you stop believing in the other, so who is to blame for the loss of happiness in our lives?

Deep inside you understand that, you can either go on loving each other or it can end like that, you are not inferior for being honest, you not inadequate for needing the other. It is a feeling you cannot satisfy yourself, a life you can't live alone, a journey you won't travel on your own. You need that someone, that you can trust, whom you know better, and love with everything that you have now, in the future, and forever, people like that just don't come around every day.

That's the catch, of thinking that you can replace someone, of lying to ourselves that ahead lays better people that will offer us a greater future. While it was all in your hands, with you every day, and you allowed it to slip away like that, you lied to yourself.

You can never harm yourself by loving your partner truly, if you do not open your heart and commit, then that is meant to hurt your soul, but if it is true love that you caring within, you will never be disappointed. Trust in love, live through it honestly in your lives, as you move on with life, you will only be able to attract a person whose willing to give in to you permanently. If one refuse to surrender themselves like you, that particular individual will disappear out of your universe of care, you need to give in with your whole heart, and never stop believing, put your faith in the other.

Continue every day to commit to your partner with everything that you are, let love be the deepest commitment you have ever made. The first thing that guarantees your safety when you wake up, cherishing someone completely. We are in a society that has compromised relationships in so many ways, yet you can carry it through.

You can only be sure of who you are, and what you're doing when you have given yourself to someone entirely. True love is not a risk that you take, it is a commitment that you make, and if you commit yourself to the other honestly, you can never go wrong. Love is trustworthy, there is something that lives in us human beings, which feeds on our heart's deepest desires, and to the other that you cherish. Then you wouldn't lose, so don't live life being afraid of heartbreaks, disappointments, and emotional breakdowns.

Trust in love, for it is a virtue, it can never lead you astray, it is something that you must have closer to your heart, like an armor, to protect you from harm, and your heart from breaking. Allowing someone to be part our lives shields our hearts from loneliness, nothing can hurt you, or harm you when true love is the center.

It is not the world which surrounds us that is liable towards loving what we are, or teaching us how to care. It is our responsibility to be giving love every day, to take on the obligation to cherish someone's presence in our lives. We must put ourselves in that position of showing passion, caring for that particular person, as it is a very important factor to reflect that kind of feeling towards your partner, and with all your heart. You can never go wrong with committing to the other, there's just no losing anything, if you feel the need to, then don't doubt yourself on any occasion.

Love holds the key to a peaceful and a happy family, you don't need, all the ups and downs of this world, you just wake up in the morning, and enjoy all of life's best moments. As for man, do not only avoid, wars in the house, and in your communions, also refrain from political affairs, that will make life easy, and loosen up on the tension, and the stress. In the relationships is all that which you must be on the lookout for permanently, why bring all this negative energy into your life?

You can argue when something provokes the anger in you, yet you mustn't entertain it, political wars have never won a family battle, it's betrayal in relationships, it will sell your soul, and your heart out to all which is vain.

If you ever find someone who is truly worth keeping closer to your heart, then stay true to that person, so much would make sense enjoying every moment with one human being. Do not avoid the responsibility of loving someone wholeheartedly, if you have never been alone, you can almost think that love will always be around.

Only after you have separated with someone that you loved deeply, that you will begin to see everything and everyone separating with you. It looks and feels very simple when you cheating on the relationship that you have, however when there's no one in your life, you begin to realize that you will not easily find anyone who can commit to you again.

I had been committed to loving someone all my life and had not yet experienced the world as a single person, and love had never dropped me. Even when I was in difficult situations, I would be nurtured by the tenderness I had in my heart, only after I decided to be on my own. Then everything turned against me, because I had made a decision to turn my back on the one I was supposed to care for, even in those situations where I would be remembered by the good of this universe. Now so much had forgotten about me, I was disappointed, from there I realized that true love could be something alive, and clearly sees and knows who serves it, and who doesn't.

I couldn't blame the universe or anyone, I had made my own decision, to stop caring for the one who valued my well-being, and to myself, and it would only be for some time. Only that, at the end, I couldn't remember how to please someone, and life had passed me with all its qualities, I had turned my back on love.

At first, I didn't mean to harm anyone, I just meant to spend some time alone, and look at myself and where I was heading with loving the other permanently, and see whether I was at the right place for commitment, or what? When you have been with a person for a longer period, there's a stage where you want to know if it could be appropriate to be fully committed to loving each other, taking the relationship to the next level.

It felt like it would be a turning point, of soul searching to connect, or find deep connections with my inner being, but little did I know that even when I wanted my way back, I couldn't find it. Life passed me, no money, or a wife, even kids, regardless of how much I needed to, it became impossible, I had turned against what was my responsibility to be a normal person. I tried by all means, only to find that there's nothing, and people are just passing, as for woman grew up stronger and older, and gave birth to children for caring men. Age and time traveled through me while I remained watching, to a point where I was forced to master my understanding, is then that I could see the light.

You cannot believe how love can be very strange, it moves along with females, no matter what life throws at you. If you remain loving, you will survive, yet if you stop caring, that would be the first time, and you had to experience how cruel the world can be, because a lot of things will come to pass. Love waits for no one, woman know better how to move with time, everything about them is to make sure that they always remember how to care. So that they mustn't let so much slip away, to be always content of the fact they are growing up too fast and they might need to see that, they live up to pace.

Women are growing up fast, they never stop for anything, and their purpose is to keep on loving a man, if you allow true love an opportunity to pass you. Then your age will leave you behind, and you will never be able to find your soul mate, someone you choose to be with as you loved and cared about them deeply.

You then have to let young man and woman of similar ages, have their own choice, and then you will follow after, which makes you the last option. While the cause of everything is just the simplest mistakes that we make, by allowing good and kind people with overflowing abundance of love, who knows how to caress someone to pass. Whereas what you need is to hold on to your lover, once you start loving, you are mostly vulnerable in spirit, you must remain within that flow of life, never get bored of caring, be true to your relationship, as well as your partner, and nothing will ever cheat you.

Of which is the thing about loving a person, you don't begin to love and then decide to stop, once you engage in a relationship, forever has just begun. You can rather stop before you can go any further or experience anything by doing so much in that part of creation. Then you are free to say I want out; I don't need my life to account for anything that I have done in this accidental communion. However, once you start doing something or everything necessary within that union of souls, then is better to stay within that commitment, loving each other truly, don't go back, keep going and see what the future holds.

It is so much that happens because we didn't understand how to resemble care, even when you want a second chance, it becomes a cycle of misfortunes that you will have to go through. It is better to have never met, or committed yourself to anyone, then life would be easy to pass through any situation and to understand whatever is going on around you. It could be because your blood hasn't started circulating, once it starts to circulate through relationships you only have love to rely on.

Hang on to love with everything that you have, and never stop resembling how important your partner is, as it is that which is our essence of creation. We don't just play with such a holy part of ourselves, as the world can never wait for one man or woman to understand how crucial being trustworthy to each other is, and how much the universe is dependent on seeing human beings moving forward with forming life.

You could have wanted to discover so much, only that to let love pass you, is like letting go of an armor which is meant for your protection. You feel as if the whole world is fighting with you, while is not, it is moving fast with people loving each other, it is beating quicker than anything you can ever understand. You have to stay in the flow of life, as true love is the wheel that spins faster than any human being can ever keep up with, without anyone to care for truly, and you can never stop this circle of creation.

People are always involved with making love to each other, and they can never stop because of anything or anyone. It takes the whole world of human beings to understand someone and stop what they're doing for one to find a room. Especially for a person who wants to come into the circle of creation; hence you must engage first before marriage.

You must learn to love with a heart that believes more in it, and better in this present age that people have begun to realize the importance of being trustworthy. Man and woman shall not be eager to deceive each other anymore, because they have now matured on issues of relationships, and no one will be fooling with another's feelings, like life used to be. It is better when you believe as you can find something that works for you, before you run out of options, into a world whereby you have been consumed by lies and deceits, as you have failed to understand how important true love is.

Have that undying faith in loving your partner, be a hero, your legend, of commitment, and difficult situations of not understanding how to care coming to pass. You belong to true love, and when you offer your deeper affections, give with an open heart, and enough to satisfy a human soul. Not to blame others for not knowing what they are doing in your life, the only thing that seeks a home is your hearts in each other. You don't have to be challenged by situations in the dark, learn to walk in a clear path, without being weary of how you do things.

Do not let an opportunity to be happy in a relationship passes you, because you can never see what your partner is doing on the other side. True love doesn't drop anyone, if your heart fears loving as you don't know whether your lover is cheating or not, you are only harming yourself. Once someone cheats on you, love will catch you, it knows and sees everything, like that, you have an armor to protect yourself with, no matter how people try to master situations that will always be available for you.

So have faith, although in a relationship trust and honesty can fade away just like that, when you can't see each other. It is only strong when your partner is around, love like that does harm an individual, but try to be strong for your partner, and have all those virtues without seeing what the other is doing.

Chapter Two

Virtues of love

Love is meant to perfect our lives, it holds the only key in unlocking the true human potential and restoring dignity among humans, and it needed everything from a person. It required a lot of hard work and dedication into caring about others. When there had been no quality of the heart, you fail to recognize true love, and most of what can change the nature of relationships is the fact that people have different activities that they are bound with. In order to succeed loving one another you need to have an understanding of what they are, you must be very concerned about each other.

Without anyone who cares and support everything that you do, your life has been interrupted in every level of creation, and all these causes certain disturbances into full development. Being committed can heal a lot in a human being and defines the role that you have come to play in this vast enormous universe. So much love has to be given to these different activities, which are necessary for both partners to find happiness in their lives. As we are here to address certain issues that have disturbed each one of us or even suffered being alone. You could have not recognized that someone is very important in making everyday a pleasure to enjoy, or value one another, with respect towards commitment.

Finding true love is something which can help to change our attitude and feelings towards other people. All of which could be caused by anything or lacking understanding in the value of life, and it would therefore become a solution to help in building and rebuilding inside our own lives, and be able to find the worth in each other's presence. I have never known the exact cause of solitude, but knew that whatever causes that, could have been a lot of negligence in dealing with human beings, and lacking good care in resembling quality of the heart in other people.

You don't have to be nice to a certain individual because you know them or you want them to be lovers with you. It is always important to resemble care and good attitude towards each and every person that you meet, something great worth living for can come out of any situation. That kind of behaviour is meant for human beings to easily relate with one another and share something deep within their soul, it is the point of attraction that connects directly with others. It is the same with every human, and one can think of that as the physical attraction only, yet it can also help in finding your soul mate, someone who can commit to you with all their heart.

Happiness can fade away when there's no love between two people, until loneliness comes and snatches you away. When there's real commitment every night and day of your lives you become very good for each other to strengthen the bond of your union. Sadness comes from lacking someone to care for, it becomes something that refuses for human beings to be free in everything that they're doing, it belittles people, ridicule them, and causing them problems that leads to lack of socialization.

There were a lot of things that had come in between our lives and being happy people, we all didn't understand at first what has happened to this current life that we living. It seems like we have found so much that is meant to lead us astray, there were things which seem to matter, and they don't, since they do not travel through the route of true commitment. Regardless of where a lot that we engage in can be heading to, when is not in the path of love, or towards finding someone who cares for you, it has no significance. What a human being needs at the end of the day is a solution that will reunite them with the ones that they long to be with the most.

With all the complications that comes with growth, there's never enough space or energy to dedicate to love. You need someone who will permanently be there for you, once you separate with that person you become miserable. Especially when you have been with each other for a very long time, sharing in moments of true love.

When the relationship has given you the best out of life, so much which happened in that communion cannot be found somewhere again. The minute you break apart with that kind of an individual, all of which you have done is buried, and you now have to create new memories. So imagine if you had been with more than one human being, with every commitment that you pass through, you lose something special.

When you have given so much of yourself, what is there left to give to someone else? It is the law of love that we cannot defy, within a loving relationship you can be able to grow into everything that you desire. When your heart has committed truly, you find strength to develop into so much that is necessary for life, until you're stronger to confront all of existence. As you begin to understand how to give what you are, to the other honestly, true love begins to restore your dignity and all the requirements of happiness that you've lost along the way, are put back the way they meant to be.

After separating with the one that you loved deeply, there are a lot of things that can come in between you and finding love again, of which you cannot understand how you ended up in that kind of situation. You will get to know a lot that you didn't even know existed before, complications that make life impossible to comprehend.

It is part of those things which you cannot know what they are and their significance, however, if they are not there, they cause weaknesses that disturbs human beings from being together. It is some of those smallest things which are taken out of a relationship, and everything becomes so uncomfortably, and they cannot be replaced easily, they're only removed and you begin to fall apart.

It was in reality where I encountered all these kinds of difficulties that no matter how strong your heart beats for a human being. You can never know what went wrong, and looking into that situation you cannot do anything about it, you just become powerless. I was searching for true love, it would mean everything for me, to once again be united with that special soul.

As I continuously failed to find the right person, I wanted to know how deep can some relationship hurt a man, or a woman, and why you just can't pick up where you left off, why do I feel deeply forsaken? What can you do with all the love that you have inside or that which you want to give, when so much outside is fighting you, not to ever get a chance to be with someone to commit to?

Everything I did was dedicated to love, but my heart had died out of loving a human being. I couldn't arrive where I can meet someone who I can give the kind of commitment that is necessary for one to be happy, and for a very long time I didn't know what I had done for me to be in this predicament.

How true love keeps on passing me, we had been from the world that knows and understand how to do things. It was in situations which explains that things are not happening by accident, and that whatever happens, is because you understand exactly how things became physical.

Where did things go wrong? I knew that it started with a simple goodbye from the one I loved, and that was the end of it, and the beginning of my loneliness. From there everything just became a huge chaos of one woman after another becoming what I didn't understand. They turned into beasts, like I was fueling them to neglect themselves like a prostitute will, all that happened because of letting go of what I had.

I wanted to know why have I entered in this nature of misunderstanding in life, I then began studying this kind of behaviour because I was growing old, and it couldn't stop, and there was nothing that I could give to someone that another wouldn't.

Then I discovered the masters of life, which became an inspiration for me to learn a lot about my deeper self, and how it can help to restore the love in you back to normal. It teaches more regarding our daily lives and how to lead yourself properly into a better direction. It came to me as a reflection of my inner being, and how important it is to understand the outcome of our actions, and what can go wrong in a relationship, which can influence your entire existence.

It emphasizes the value of things, how to care for something special, and that nothing can ever break unless it has been misused. This is how we end up in situations, that we don't know how to come out of, and we linger there with no way out. Of which could be the results of how we don't realize the significance of doing things the way they needed to be done, and fail to exercise caring for the worth we have in our lives.

The masters of life deals with the confrontation of things, according to how they have happened, and how to fix them. It further explains everything that is necessary for someone to find happiness. At times when you don't understand why you keep failing, it could be that you have fallen on the wrong side of creation. Where so much is no longer what you use to know, and that changes the nature of all that we see as the results of who we are.

I had spent years not understanding where I am, and how I ended up there, it could have started as a breakup, however, I was snatched by time and consumed by situations, and it ended up as loneliness. It was then that I began to realize that I am alone and lost in affection, and how everything I touch keeps breaking. That's how far love had gone with me, after separating with the one I had loved so deep, you can never know what will happen in the future.

Which is the reason why one might need to arrive at the deepest level of their understanding, you don't know how bad the damage could be, and you might think you are alone, yet there are others who have gone through the same situation. Some could have find their way back, and others didn't, and part of who they are remains in spirit as a formation of this world, it eventually disturbs people from finding a way to breakout of their self-imprisonment without searching for themselves deeper.

Like they are left in spirit to tell a story through experience, of how far life can go with you, if you ever abandoned the necessities of creation and love. Everything that we are in this world forms some part of reality that can disturb human beings when they are not where they're supposed to be.

For everything that we do, and all that we are, there's always a masters of life, and it will always be watching over us, and is here to force the essential truth and honesty out of our entire being. These are laws of creation that have always watched over everything, and not only are they guarding over you, but they are safekeeping the whole of humanity.

We always get what we worth, and when we fail to live life accordingly then there's nothing that we deserve from this beautiful creation. This is where we learn that there are no accident, that things are not happening by chance, it is always meant to be like that. When you have failed the laws of nature, you're being punished for it, everything binds deeper than our own will.

So it becomes what you must live to understand, that our lives are under the control of an entity bigger than ourselves, and to make it worse is that, no one ever knows that there is something that could be watching over us. You only begin to see that things are not right, when your well-being has collapsed, and by then it could be too late because we are never taught about this kind of situations. It works to control the outcome of life in the favor of those who have done everything accordingly, and what if you have overlooked the rules of humanity, you live according to your understanding.

Virtues of love are some of the most important things in a relationship, they make everything work like it should, and they are there to create harmony within our lives, honors the true union of hearts, and blesses the love and all that has brought human beings together. It creates peace, sense of belonging, the need to give to each other every day, and reassurance for the commitment that has united the couples in one.

These are some of the most crucial things that you can lose when you've separated with someone who had loved and given in to you. Things can become difficult to maintain, and it might take so much that you have to once again find a communion that is worth living for.

Love when has become what it must be, created not by our ignorance, but our willingness to do more for what we have, without pride and ego standing in our way. When you have true value for what you've been blessed with, a relationship cannot be difficult to maintain, from not having much, to understanding, acceptance, reliability, growth, let us grow together, and pass situation as one heart. Something important has brought us to finding one another, and we value and accept that about the other, and tolerate in each other.

More than everything that there is, there's that thing which you give to one another, you must prepare yourself to bring that quality of life and love into a communion. Whether is easy for a man or woman, you need to be prepared to learn about this kind of things. Let one be natural when it comes to loving and committing the way it must be done, a good, worthwhile relationship needs no one to compromise his or her happiness. You must just be able to give all that you are into someone, without caring how much you have given.

You don't have to worry like you surrendering yourself into the emptiness, you giving in true love, where you need no reason why you have to give your life. Rejoice about letting go of who you are, it always works both ways, and to appreciate, let the other knows how much you value them. There could have been situations where one can think that maybe you thought less of the other, but no, you highly regard each other the way you must, a good relationship it's a two-way channel, where energy to love flows.

It is our only gift to inner happiness, if you can't give in to someone, then there won't be any reason necessary for you to understand why you must surrender yourself. We always require that much from each other, no matter who you are, you might need a little bit of honesty and integrity, because you won't fall for a human being that you know.

True love is the stranger that we allow into our lives, you trusting your happiness in the hands of a person that you have never known. Regardless of how much you have, the presence of another must be valued with all that you are. Do not look away in a situation to commit, be always present, as you can never know the other's intentions.

What makes love what it is, a pleasure for someone to be around you, honesty and trustworthiness, is everything that makes a relationship to be a joy for the other to be with you. The thing is that you can never have the same person every day, who loved you with all that they had. That is what makes that special human being who has given in to you, worth being valued, as you cannot have that similar human every day. If you ever find the one who respects you, then you must hold on tight to that individual, as you might not have another again.

So much changes with every situation, but these are the only treasures of life worth sacrificing ourselves for, as they remain the same, to love and to value a human being, is what creates happiness for someone that will last forever. You spend the rest of your existence searching for something that you had, which you didn't care of, and you ask yourself why didn't I have what I wanted, or everything I needed. However, whom can you blame when at some point you have overlooked carrying, and an opportunity for the other to be happy with your presence in their lives.

When love was still there, you had every day to spend with someone, yet overlooked that chance to give the best of your deepest self, and treasured that with every beat of your heart. You don't have to miss an opportunity to love, it is not to be misused, be always content in a loving situation, and take everything deep into consideration.

Do not let any moment pass you, because you might allow your greatest life to have passed you. I always regret not getting the best out of a relationship, however when you have given everything that you are at first, when commitment still mattered more than anything.

Then you don't have to die for you to regret what you come to lose, when you know that in a relationship you have given everything that you have. Love can never let you down, when you have offered the best of your abilities to loving someone, to have committed yourself spiritually and physically. You only need to remember that true love doesn't drop anything, it always catches everyone who sought after it, with all that they are.

Chapter Three

Elements of love

Then comes the breakup, every separation is caused by a certain fight between two people, yet at times is not the war which we fighting that matters, it is the battle inside our soul. It is better if you both align with life, however, given the circumstances of the world we live in, the eternal connection that exists within lovers.

It is just safe to remain in your relationship, loving each other truly. How can you ever connect to love again, after separating with the one who had ever cared for you? That is likely to be the issue that we go through, from breaking apart with our loved ones, you only have so many opportunities to find true love.

From when love has disappeared where it used to be true, you begin to feel as if the world around has turned against you, and you know what has changed everything to oppose you. What insists on holding someone back? Is not about who moves on first, is the moments we've shared together. It is never easy to find a replacement for a person you've loved like that, because of the deep connection that still exists between two people that have cared for each other deeply. After a long term relationship that has exchanged so much, true love will rather hold on to yesterday than to move forward just like that.

The depth of true love is found within a long-standing relationship that has had so much memories to share. Indulge in a shared commitment, made good love so simple, and deep until it creates a bond with both the lovers, longing for them to give in to the other a little bit more, that's how people commit to each other.

There is something that we exchange, or give to each other that we both are dependent on, to be able to move forward with life normally, and at the same pace with everything. When you have been loving each other every night and day, you get to understand that, relationships are protected by a certain entity that we share deep within our soul. Is only when you lack true love that you can think something that real to who we are, doesn't exist, given that once you've failed to find that nature of understanding, you cannot just undo what you have become.

Within a loving relationship our lives are strictly protected from outside interference, so that we can move forward within that flow of life. That kind of interaction with one another prevents a human being from intercepting with that cycle of love. We become cycled by a strong bond of true love, when things begin to fall apart, it is our own doing that opens the gates to intruders by lacking commitment in our communion.

Daily the reason for resembling trustworthiness to your partner, could be to fulfill the will of creation. Which in some way, is trying hard to exercise caring, for which you are, until you become familiar with loving that person and remaining loyal. You gain each other's commitment, trust, and build on love, an honest relationship it's a resting place where you can rest your life, or be able to lean on.

If you ever find it difficult to understand it right, or very well, it matters more than all there is, to know exactly how to care for something important in our daily existence. What is the function of love, controlling everything in our lives? It is an idea of creation that is motivated by happiness, which you see human beings begin to follow, and therefore creating a way of life, and that is true love that they possess for one another.

Love exists in a situation of life that has been created by two people who have truly dedicated their lives, and bodies to pleasing one another truthfully. True love is the area which they have chosen to practice their understanding of the world, their center of creation. That kind of commitment becomes the genuine foundation of everlasting happiness, something that human beings mustn't overlook, if they want to discover their worth.

At some point, I had found myself in a situation that would offer me an opportunity to reunite with my inner self again, by enabling me to work into a certain area that would allow falling in love easy. Deep within my head I was keen on finding a good partner, and I kept on looking for one, however, I was searching at the wrong place, a worthwhile relationship was in another level where I didn't even need to be very concerned about it, only needed to focus so that whatever comes my way, I would be prepared and able to handle.

I eventually lost everything because of how I didn't understand what I was doing. I stopped focusing on my objectives, and became obsessed with finding someone to love me, and that led me to deeply neglecting the responsibilities, which I was supposed to take. Yes to be in a relationship is something that I couldn't find easy in me, yet at times it could be the environment where you are, that could be able to offer you an opportunity to meet the right person, who can give themselves to you openly.

As a human being searching for a worthwhile relationship, you could need to always be prepared, so that whenever true love comes, finds you in a good condition and ready to commit. We are sometimes crown for our efforts, and it could be very important not to search for a partner to be with. However, fix your life so that when someone to love appears, finds you in a state that welcomes them in your care.

What influences the nature of how we know things is separation, how it affects one, and the way it can turn into a life situation that cannot be resolved easily. That effect of losing the love of your life, it destroys everything that one has ever known, and for a very long time is all that you will want to pass. Without having to mention so much, that stage of losing someone you loved truly, is only made to be understood through your own experience.

When I lost someone long ago, I felt love for everything being the only way in which I can restructure myself back to normal. Somehow I knew that I needed to surrender who I am to whatever could arouse that kind of feeling in me. You cannot sustain yourself in this world without anything to hold on to, you need to give your heart to something. We forever feel the need to offer ourselves like that, being the only way to survive all that is happening around us and be human again.

When you learn to harvest the good you have in your heart, it could be able to heal all the pain that you feel inside. Though you might not fall in love instantly, yet you are able to earn your life back, the hurt mustn't push you to live in denial of who you are. From what you have harvested there will be something that comes back as true love at a certain point, and in a way that could be able to make you happy, unlike allowing the loss to ruin your whole entire being.

Then there was the part where I had discovered a way to rehabilitate myself from all that had happened. When you find yourself inside, it feels so strong, as if the feeling could be attached to loving a human being, but when there's no one to commit to, how will you handle that? You start to realize that it takes time for that nature of loss to heal. When you begin to feel everything within you, it becomes something that could be associated to reuniting with someone like that, as a way to complement your happiness.

Little does it exist that it is love, yet it is only meant to heal yourself back to being content again, and be redeemed from what you have gone through, to normal once more. As you keep flowing with everything, true love will find you along the way, and as for the feeling that you experiencing, has more to do with loving who you are, as well as other human beings. Giving justice to your actions, and describing the nature of what you feel, as to where do it fit in altogether.

You are rehabilitating yourself from all the mistakes that you've made, things you did that you know very well have repercussions, and if you don't make that right, you will forever suffer that setback. Love does not exist in relationships only, there are a lot of human beings who need the attention and being cared for out there, and to be able to see that. You must possess quality in your heart, and not that of people who don't know how to give openly, and do the right thing.

You must also learn how to love generally, and do well all the time, hatred causes one to lose focus on human beings, and begin to create a world that is full of deception, that seeks to destroy everything out there. So a lot of care is needed into this kind of life, to be able to come out of every situation as a brand new person.

To have true value in yourself, can help you to focus on creating a lot of good, however, when you look, it only resembles the love you have for life. One thing that you have to understand is that it becomes like this every day, that you have to be out there showing this kind of understanding for what you're doing.

To show compassion must come as a daily thing, or a duty towards the obligation that you have taken with yourself. The love for everything, I always say that is about caring, if you don't care about a person, then you don't possess that quality in you, it is the concrete foundation to fullness of life. You must learn to live well with other people, and be able to get along with everyone peacefully. In a way that you're open to ideas and suggestions, exercise kindness until you become a joy to be around.

To me life has reached a stage whereby a human being doesn't have to seek forever. Even if situations can be difficult, let there be a way in which someone can at least rejoice in this present existence, do not allow them to die without satisfying part of their needs. Love has formed as a very important component that has been used to create the world, as well as it has a very important role to play in our daily basis, and through it you're able to find a way to touch lives.

As there is no other way in which you can reach people's lives, except for the fact that it has been the point of contact. Without it in whatever you do, the quality of life has been compromised, and there is nothing left in that part of creation. You need to understand, as to how we end up with no option, except to give in to it, as our only way out.

Trust is another important thing that you should have for both of you, it is something that must be available within two people that have come together in the union of hearts. A lot of things can come in between to ruin the happiness that exists for lovers, you can never find peace if you don't have faith in your partner. It is just a waste of time to think that you can be happy, not being sure that your lover feels the same way about maintaining trustworthiness within the relationship that you have.

There is no way that you can find peace if you are not sure of what your partner is doing, love is built on trust. I don't know what is there left between two people, if you don't have that virtue of commitment in your relationship. When you lack that mutual believe in one another, everything has been taken away from your union, you cannot live with someone knowing that you not content of what they're doing. True love dwells within human beings that have decided to do justice for themselves, trusting each other is the basic understanding to discovering more greatness that exists within ourselves.

Honesty as well can play a very important role in your lives, by making sure that you don't have a thing to hide from each other. Living everyday openly to one another, without the need to be keeping anything from your partner, you are welcoming the other into your life completely. Although it is difficult to be open with everything, you must try to find an angle to deal with things. The sooner you start talking, the better chances you have of clearing things out of your way.

Do not keep any secrets from each other, be it that you just encountered a certain disturbing person, or an idea that could want to change your lives or who you are. You don't have to grow a thing that is not necessary for your well-being, make sure you do not allow anything or anyone to plant a seed in your heart. The minute something tries to come in your life, share it with your partner so that you can win together as mates, and always remember that a good team doesn't lose.

So you not only playing for your partner, however, you're in it for each other, so that you can protect what has brought you together, something that can slip away from you unexpectedly like that. It goes beyond just the ordinary circumstances that you don't know or see what the next day might turn out to be. So you keep upfront and closer to each other, by not allowing anything to come in between you and ruin what you have already, as secrets can distance you from one another.

Do not settle for anything less than what you need or really want, it's a relationship meant for two people to share in the joy of their lives. Always keep your needs satisfied both ways, and if you not, don't deny yourself the truth by saying out loud, so that you all are welcome and catered for in this communion.

Respecting one another can make a huge difference, by knowing that there are things which you wouldn't do or say to your partner, and keep it like that as well, whether they are around or not. One doesn't have to see you to practice good morals, knowing very well that everything we do impacts on the kind of behaviour that you will resemble towards the other. You need to be prepared to behave properly, and give love that is necessary.

Life is something that could be lived anyhow, best to have lived it, loving someone and treasure every moment that you share with that special person. It all pays out very well at the end, to be full of respect for one another, and give love like you suppose to. Some mistakes can disturb your progress in all levels of your creation, and without you understanding what has happened, you look behind and begin to realize that it cannot be undone.

You can try to rectify that, only to find that you can never go back to that time, when you still knew how to be a very good human being, one who knows how to do things for true love. Everyone that you allow in your life changes so much.

Love isn't the same as fashion, is good when it is as original as it was from creation, there's something special about true love that doesn't disappear. It has a tradition of giving, receiving, and exchanging with each other what we are, that custom of who we are mustn't stop bearing fruits in our lives, and when there's nothing left to give, what do you exchange with one another?

Could have achieved so much in life, and along the way when I had thought to myself, that I deserved everything the world has to offer. I felt another mountain standing before me and my destiny, love had stood in the path I wanted to travel through to success, and with all the challenges that I have never met.

Even if I could try to force my way through, deep down inside, I knew that this means I have to be over-prepared for everything that I will come across, or else I would have to accept that I failed to find love. I couldn't compromise my objectives to marry someone special no matter what, even if I wanted to, that had been taken out as an option for me.

Born in a certain time in a world where the truth and love mattered more than anything, and I had chosen this path for myself, and it was not a life for so many. However for those who are prepared to participate in creation, and commitment unconditionally, giving all that they are to loving human beings, and the other without compromising what they are.

It so much that we mean by love and caring for someone, what do you find acceptable in a human being? I have discovered in me something that deeply yearns for true love, and it won't settle for anything less. Somehow I opened my heart and believe that I have found who I am truly, love ruled at the center of my entire being, and I had to work my way from that point of understanding, into the world, learning to confront things from that angle.

With love like that, at first I felt so lost in the world where I was birthed, I then realized that to be born with a free mind and a loving heart is not a crime. We all belong somewhere, and no matter what we say about ourselves to other people, we have a special place, where our ideas belongs. We serve a unique purpose, and with true love, we will come out forth, and nobody said that the suffering was going to last.

I had love for life, and everything seeking freedom out of me into existence through that path of true love, and if the universe couldn't give me what I needed. I wanted to leave this world the way I came, because there was no way I could change who I am.

Chapter Four

Slice of life

We are introduced to reality at different levels, you can live for a very long time not being aware of where you are spiritually. When you begin to be conscious, you start to realize who and where you are, and maybe things could be worse, however, is better than not knowing or remaining behind forever.

Even if plans can be invented to try and close the gap that time can have over your life when you're lost. There could be situations that you cannot pass very well with your mind instantly. You might need to labor very hard to understand things the way they are, for you to have clarity over everything that is happening in your life and around you.

I was a plan for myself to find solutions in everything that had happened in my life, against all odds. How do we reunite with ourselves in a better way, when love has left us torn apart? I wished that we didn't have to learn how to take control over so much that we engage in, that whatever you do impacts back to you. Only that if you choose a good way to live through, nothing could ever work for you, that's how I felt at some point.

At times when things happen, you might think that it is normal, then after some time you begin to realize that the world isn't how you thought of it to be. A lot of what we know is not how it is, so much is not based in honesty, sometimes things occur because there is no alternative. Yet if there's another route that will enable human beings to live well, even if you have to change current situations and the way things are being done, for life to be better, then why not do it?

You do things right and competent, hoping that everything in your life would be going back to normal, and no one would be granted favors over you. That the world would just be an open platform to move through, however, it doesn't happen like that. You begin to realize that a lot is not happening accordingly, that we could be in a period whereby so much is not based on merit.

There could be a need for something more, and that as people we have done everything that we could, to prove our worth, but that was not enough. Regardless of how you keep trying, it doesn't work, and in all that you remain alone, without anyone to care for you. To succeed it needed a lot of faith, do you believe in what you're doing, and loyalty, are you loyal to whatever you want?

There is so much that you understand is not being done accordingly, everyone has their purpose and objectives with their lives, and how they want to see things happen. At times they insist to have their own way even if it is against all that we are, and the love we have for life, and for each other as human beings. Is about what you know, who knows how to influence situations wants his will to take place, and in the favor of what they strive to master, is how they let things be done, and be given in abundance.

It explained a lot about why we went through a stage of life's biggest misunderstanding, we lived in a world where we thought that we mattered, and somehow we didn't. We wondered why we didn't matter, regardless of how hard we try to involve ourselves with everything, we kept on failing. We were just workers with no compensation, and we couldn't get to the part where what we do is taken into consideration.

Then at the end, I somehow began to understand that maybe not anyone deserves a favor, and there's none who has ever been granted one. Its hard work, and patience that people have succeeded through, and when you haven't arrived there or gone beyond that surface, you will think life is unfair.

In some other situation we are required to understand something more, or master our own lives, in order to be content of everything that is happening. You could find yourself lost when you haven't understood anything, however, to be satisfied with what you doing creates a way or an order for life to be progressive. You establish a path that you must learn to follow or live through, this is a route designed by your understanding that leads to your destiny.

You become so sure of what you doing that is not something you can easily change about yourself, unless you're standing at a place where the path is questionable. You develop an idea that is of major concern or a part of life that cannot be kept forever, which must be lived. A truth that cannot be concealed, a route that must be followed, this is where life could begin to make sense for a lot of people.

You play a role in creation and towards creating a certain world, that even before you could arrive there, through the difficult stages, you understand why you have to work hard, and what to get from it. You strive for you to be content with everything, you become a true servant, working for your slice of life. In a world controlled by something bigger than what you are, if you want your will to happen, then there is no other way.

You have to work within these times, understand why you need to start somewhere, you labor knowing that you want situations to change in your life, and be better. Though it can be difficult at the beginning as everything could be against the life that you live. Maybe you are not completely opposed where you have duties and obligations to fulfill, however, in your physical being, it gets bitterer as you try to move forward into a greater place.

So as you go through a period of no hope, you wonder what I would do with the remaining of my life, if I don't pass what I seek to understand. Because time can ruin a person's future, as you experience delays. You can try to blame people for refusing to support all your efforts with love, only that when you work tirelessly without ever giving up, things do change at some point, and at the end you do achieve your goals.

Even if the whole world can refuse to let you in, however, with a good idea you can change the universe, and your platform will be created for you to live through. Which will allow every individual to understand you and be able to thrive within that opportunity, which you have created for yourself. As you can be left back for a long time, and a lot can become meaningless and only remaining with how you want to see things happen.

Irrespective of whether you are weary or not, from the obstacles of creativity, you must get up and move forward, you could arrive at a certain place whereby life offers too much or even more. Though it might feel like the cost is too high, as you are required to work hard, you are prepared for it, and that commitment deserves a break.

At times as you wonder, you know that regardless of what the universe can throw at me, I don't need to try hard and fit into situations. Yet so much could be said every day, that if there's no way to come back from being forsaken by the world, take any way available, but you would rather hold on to what you want and the way you must, the rest doesn't matter.

I was offered things in a very strange way as a young man, and I had find it hard to understand the reason for all that. Our paths of life are sometimes designed to push us to have certain knowledge of the world, you can never know everything you need to reach your destiny. Though you could find happiness at the level of forcing things to happen, and you can be able to manifest a lot of what you've been thinking from that.

However, it might not be what you require to get where you need to, so do not hate the universe when you cannot see everything that you desire, life has its lesson and matters the most to whatever is necessary. No matter how difficult situations create themselves, it could be that you need to learn about finding a way to add value to humanity.

Once a certain way of life had formed through deception, and deceived human beings and they became so lost, and others didn't know what to do. Life had changed somewhere so deep, and so many felt dictated by that path of existence, because everyone was needed to do one thing. In reality it can be difficult to adjust to a brand new attitude, it is just not easy, how can one change to something different overnight.

There was something that carried value in deception, and it affected human beings deeply, as people can do anything when their lives are compromised. So much out there can try to devour the world of love, given that failure to understand modernization and the time in which we live in, can lead human beings to try and change things, where it mustn't be changed. Yes we can understand how to do so much, only that you don't have to do everything because it can be done.

With time people have discovered a lot that can deceive human beings, things that can affect a person living life normally, and everyone can be affected by such a thing. So how do you know that what you doing is worth your efforts or not, is true love. Love justifies our actions and who we are, yes we want to see change, yet we don't want to be changed where we have loved.

We lived at the edge where if you don't watch out for your well-being, life could turn anyone into something worthless, and you could find yourself being a victim of such a thing, when trying to apply your knowledge to be a part of existence. The world works for human beings to be normal, however, for those who refuse to have taken the ordinary path, things could turn out to be very difficult.

To influence reality is something else, whatever it is that human beings try to put out there, whether good or bad, there will always be someone who responds to that. Is how people become part of so much, even if not many, but that specific number, and we witness a lot of this kind of behaviour as the world keeps evolving every day. As you constantly refuse to take responsibility for your own life, you're continuously being pulled to whichever direction, and if there's no one who sees into your well-being, you end up doing whatever pleases you.

We continuously see things happening but without understanding what it means. How does one become part of so much that doesn't benefit who they are, yet keeps pulling them into the dark? And you are not deceived, everyone is given enough chance to do right, we ruin our own well-being, knowing very well that our lives had been innocent. You allow situations to turn you into something that you not, and you know you're being influenced by human beings and conditions.

Asked whether people understand themselves without anything interfering in their lives? If the stage was set like that for everyone to be responsible of their well-being, can they fully take charge of who they are? For some time the platform was left free to understand if human beings can take control of their own welfare and handle their affairs very well.

For a very long time I couldn't be physically responsible for my own well-being, left alone I did whatever I wanted, which was good, though it leaves you with a lot of stigma. So to derive meaning can become a very shameful thing, without the outside world interfering in our lives. I had never trusted my life in the hands of other human beings,

I had studied young on my own, and created my ideas into physical form. That had led me to discover my way of doing things at a very early age, and after that, I have been listening to being creative and leaving my life from that, so yes I don't know what it means to be influenced by other people and situations.

Therefore at the end of the day we can have a mutual agreement, and say that human beings need understanding. They want to be shown the way out of situations, in which they could be stuck, hence we require proper guidance, education, and consultation. So yes it hasn't happened in our lives from the beginning of time, to find ourselves in a situation where we had been freed, where we are normally good and it is in this greatness that we have now come to understand our lives.

So regardless of how things have changed, people need to understand what it means to be human and being good. Though we have come to the beginning of a new era, where we believe that so much is meant to change. We still don't know what do we owe to this most unpleasant way of life, which to some is the only thing to live for, maybe we owed it to success, and in that manner, we will be able to physically move forward into a better direction.

Now the time has come for us to discover so much about our entire existence, this is a stage where it matters to find true love about ourselves, and forget the ways that seeks to rule by ruining people's understanding. Yet it is a call of being a man to discover new ways of doing things when the time has come, and you must get up and go out there to lead the way. However, you must always remember that human beings are about the most important things in life, how to find true love that exists deep within their soul, which is what everyone want to see creating in their lives.

We need to see a universe with good morals being what people strive to create, because now is the time to make sure that we live our lives to the best of our abilities, and be able to take responsibility for some of our actions. Yes it is a world where you have to play your part, if you want to witness what you want coming to life, but you must be sure it is a worthy path that you travel, so that you don't find something unworthy standing in your way towards reaching your true purpose.

Unlike in the past, man of today are required to think about what they need to achieve, as you won't have anything necessary done for you automatically. To witness the wonders of this beautiful land and the time we live in, we have to be responsible for our lives and happiness, and whatever idea you have can make a lot of sense, and create an impact on a broader perspective.

So as people we are needed to find a way on how to be creative, and how to change things for the better, as a human impact can be huge in this age that we live in. Therefore we need to learn how to create so much with love, knowing that every person can take a stand and they can disturb something very important.

That explains the effect of the world that we see on a daily basis, how so much is just design to disturb human progress, and now for the first time, in the history of our lives we could arrive. Unlike how we find ourselves stuck at the center of life, from some ideas that are created with no care for humanity. We can value these human beings that we are right now, and protect the love we have by creating well in the world.

Even if it means that we device something that humanity is not yet content of, we shift our focus from the chaotic to the most peaceful creation. Understand that people deserve better, they don't need to be exposed, as you know their presence may not be repeated, we only have one opportunity to live life well.

So from the good hearts a world of love has been created, which will protect human beings from everything, which can attempt to harm a human soul, and now things have change for the better, and beyond what so many can understand. We began from a violent era, it changed with time, from one thing to another, and people were able to lead each other through the stages of civilization. With every step we take forward things transformed, now we have emotional battles that we fighting, for us to find peace and love, and be content with everything that we have.

The situations that we facing today, are never the same as those that have occurred in the past, things have changed. People are about quality life, love, and happiness. That's how far we have been able to move forward with time. So all that which is meant to add that kind of good impact on human lives has got to live, and we can say goodbye to that old world where we lived in lack. So let's hope that we can achieve our aim of being joyful, and loving each other truly, which is the solution to human being's daily activities, and passing through these emotional battles that we face.

To some people it has been a very long and disappointing period, however, if you can create good, they can finally understand themselves, because you're doing things to bring hope. Being confident that creating wonders is just part of your responsibilities, and when you do it, you always aiming at adding proper impact, and you do it well and for all the right reasons. Everyone has their part to play in this gigantic universe, and you must make it happen in a way that is meant to be, by resembling caring for everything that lives out there, and strive to make a difference where you're mostly needed.

That's how much is required from anyone, to show everything that you're capable of. Do not hold back, or look down on something that you know could have saved a lot of human beings, and for a very long time it would have brought a positive change in people's lives. When so much has been done for you, everything feels so easy, but when one day it becomes your turn to make things happen, even if is not on the same occasion, however, only where you can make a difference, and that's all that is needed from you.

It becomes so heavy on you, like you have been asked to make a sacrifice, and you feel so strained by the part where the world is dependent on you to pass through the faced situation. Yet you can try to avoid that path, only that it could be the only way by which you as well must come back to reality, and be recognized for something, and feel the glory of leading the way in society. Life was good, the world had traveled deep, disappeared from what we expected and what we use to know, into a new universe that has become bold, in the acts of the new century. Then you ask yourself as you have been left back in the world hoping that you can make a change.

Can you add a good impact in this vast creation? Maybe you can, when true motivation exists in you, and you have the goal, vision, and determination, to go beyond your call of duty, you exceed your required expectations to reach your desires. You who carry the objective becomes the visionary, of the work fully required to be done by man, where he knows what he is doing, and that's all that is required of you to give.

One said, "Not just the slice, but the whole cake", and life will forever be better for human beings. When you know everything, then give all that you have, don't hold anything back, when something is required from you, stick to what the true motivation is, and don't keep limiting yourself to a certain point.

By giving a little of who you are, just for you to move from one point to another, you compromise things because you want to figure out a way on how to benefit your own well-being. That is how it must be for so many who cannot comprehend, but if you understand, why not do what is needed for everyone?

Sometimes you are only required to give just a little part of your understanding, or expertise to add to what is currently available, from who you are, we only require a certain aspect of your knowledge. What is the true motivation thereof? Is it about making an impact or changing lives for the better, if that is what is needed of you, what could be the real motive, and what if you know everything? Then give them all that you capable of, instead of holding human beings back, because that is what is the solution at the end, to life, you, and everyone.

Chapter Five

Love Intuition

We don't know who we are, the origin of man and woman before Christianity, which is what we are called, and where we find ourselves living our lives every day. You wake up daily, and they ask of your religious identity, and all we say is that we are Christians. We don't know why we are only acceptable as that, but is how we have been identified and recognized, as something that cannot change about the people that we are.

From our early ages we grew up without responsibilities, or just to realize that we can ruin our lives or seed of love. Especially for the male, we fail to understand what so much is meant by the earliest education that man and woman have received from birth. The simplest rule about fornication, and when we have forgotten about that, we begin to grow out of Christianity. That's the beginning of a human being losing his religious identity, and later in life, as you mature, you are required to account for all that.

This is where a lot of us got stuck, after we have lost our purity and validity, towards a law that was put before every individual and for it to be strictly obeyed. Then later you begin to question your direction in the path you have chosen, what happened to me, why can't I find someone who is willing to commit?

That's when you come back years after you have fornicated as man or woman all your lives, and that is according to the rules of religion. You never knew where you were headed, you just thought to yourself, is life, wherever is heading, it doesn't matter, and it felt so great having to live everyday like that, living without any responsibilities.

That's where or how we made simple mistakes as we began engaging in relationships early, while we were growing up, in different schools and institutions of higher learning. Where we met as young people that wanted to get closer to each other so badly, and share what we are deep within us, something that yearns to celebrate our youth.

Then as you grow older, you begin to long for true love, as you are now eager to settle. Only to find that you are no longer welcome within the cycle of love, because according to Christianity you have committed adultery. Then life begins to be very difficult from the situation you find yourself in.

One might think, "I would have forced my way back to the center of life, how would one know what I have done that is so bad". The love intuition, true love is something alive, and exists with knowledge about our past lives, mistakes, and everything that we do, about who we are, and what we have done so far. You look for someone in every part of the world, and when you can't find that special person, you keep asking yourself, what's wrong with what I am, why can't I meet anyone who's willing to commit or settle down with me?

Then it comes back to what we did all our lives, how we engaged with each other from early ages. Whichever offense you have committed in the dark, you now must account for it in the light of the day, in true love you have been marked invalid. This is where we have spent most of our lives as human beings, trying to figure out who we are, and what we've done wrong. Not that we lame or maybe we don't understand what we doing, however, we have been caught in an illegal act, being the misconduct of love.

We all know what we've been doing, yet some are not aware that what they did is not right, and continue to live without knowledge of what it is, that is a problem with the life they're living. You do realize that you have a lot of difficulties where true love is the concern, only that you don't know what you've done wrong.

Our lives in love are governed by faith and religion, depending on how you have behaved, you will be judged based on that, and it will determine the kind of person that you will meet. As someone to spend the rest of your life with you, and you know that about yourself as well, that you need someone who still has value to be loved.

It could be a difficult concept to understand, hence at some point I had defined being wise as something that you don't need to be taught. You know that doing this is wrong, and did everything to avoid it, in your head you understood it clearly without being told that this is bad. Regardless of what your friends did, you never became part of, and you grew up very well, and avoided a certain lifestyle that would stand in your way in the future. You created a path for yourself where you live without having to argue with life or anyone.

That's intelligence or to be a wise person, to avoid something that would undermine your own will in the future. Being able to understand that you need to get to a certain age where you can be sure of what you doing, you therefore avoided all the mistakes a man or a woman can ever make in one life. According to me it's a good thing given the circumstances that we usually make a lot of mistakes from engaging in relationships too early. For someone to have engaged in loving activities more than it is required of one at that age.

Meaning that if all of this was law, then it is here to reflect on the kind of a person that you would become. It resembles the nature of the human being that you are, given that you still have a long way ahead of you, or maybe you can remain trustworthy to one partner. In my opinion the ones that have passed, are those who didn't need to be taught how to be good people, however, felt it in them that it is better to stay focused.

Do not do anything too early that you might regret along the way, because when we are through with everything, our worthiness comprises of all that we have done from the beginning of our lives. Even if you passed your education very well, but failed that lesson of love, you are considered a failure.

Failing a life lesson degrades a human being far too deep, and that can affect everything that you value, and you might be left with no option except that you must accept the outcome of your present situation. That is how a lot of human beings have failed themselves, they have fail to understand how to be good Christians that knows and treasure how to behave accordingly.

It feels so unfair to so many people how things can happen, to study all your life only to be failed by something that you did in the past. Reflecting how you overlooked the greatest knowledge available to humanity, and that restrains you from exercising anything that could lead to happiness. That has in turn led to a lot of human beings living according to their own will, even if it means they settle for something which isn't true love.

They continue their existence outside the law of love, because at the end is not everybody who is curious about how things would have been, living by the law of religion and seeking after true love. Whatever is life to them is good, if is moving forward is enough, as long as it gets them to where they wanted to be. For so many to be judged for everything they have done from the beginning of their lives, feels like too much to handle.

Yet some have realized an opportunity from the path that is being lived in this new age, and have created their own understanding on how life should be. How people must proceed with finding a way on how to be content with themselves, when so much regards them invalid, from how they have behaved.

That is what has become the alternative, life outside religious laws, people mastering their own way of thinking and creating their destiny, even if is against everything that the world is. At the end when you look at what is being lived out there, you begin to understand that is not meant for so many or everyone, and we linger everywhere unable to find ourselves at the center of creation. Wondering about what could have been our greatest path, yet lost, if only I didn't choose to do things outside the sacred law, so much would've been better, and now I'm living to pay the price.

Then from years of being lost and studying thoroughly we have discovered Sikhism, a way of life that comes after we have failed to be Christians. Not like what everyone invents as a path for their own benefit, a route for those who didn't realize that their ways of doing things are wrong. Is not like choosing your own understanding to be how you live your life, an alternative for those who are still prepared to be discipline, who feel like if they should have known better, they would still be living under oath.

Sikhs became the rescue, in terms of forgiving those who never realized everything written in the scripture is meant to be followed. That fornication or adultery is a crime that you will live to pay the penalty for the rest of your entire existence.

Though there are few people who acknowledges to be lost with no clear path, who refuses to give in to other forms of beliefs, or to whatever is available out there. Who would rather hang in there and struggle with all of life than to mislead their purpose just like that. However, for those who believe, through this sacred path they can repair the damage that creation can have over our lives when confused.

So much could go wrong in our daily well-being, when you are not within a belief that governs your understanding in this vast creation. You could need to have faith and focus channeled on a certain discipline to come out of this dark hole, where we have lived without true love forever.

For those who had been lost our new discipline would be Sikhs, a way for those who never realized how important devoting yourself to true love is. It is meant to restore and teach about love, life, and happiness in the believe that we have cultivated, especially in the pursuit of knowledge, and the value of common sense. It appreciates the learning, transforms the experience into motivation heading towards a better direction, and how to live well here at the center of creation.

These are some of the most important things that you can undermine, when you looking at life from a distance. However, when you get in touch with reality and begin to involve yourself with love, you realize how lost we are, without it where is true. To be closer to true love and devotion, to care and have value for a human, being dedicating to pleasing someone who becomes part of you. Appreciating the opportunity to give what you are to a special individual, who indulges in your presence in their lives, and through that nature of commitment, living happily ever after.

Years after man and woman have passed through these institutions of learning, they begin to understand their exposure to reality. For some it could become very difficult to ever find love, real commitment that everyone is looking for, to be settled. After Christianity has shut its doors human beings are lost, and everything is just vain, nothing is ever real in your life and in that world. You search for someone, and all that you find is people who are not into committing towards true love.

There is none in that universe, and nothing in between, like it has been said, we have fail to love, and have been denied to find our place in that world of true love. So many have only begin now to see the light through Sikhs, it was then when they realize that is about discipline, and from that sacred path you're able to be content again. Outside the way of life it is just darkness that people experience, and not a thing is blessed.

In my life I had not found any meaning towards a worthy relationship, and things were not how they were supposed to be, whatever I would encounter was not meant to last forever. All that you find in between was just made for you to keep losing more of who you are, it wasn't the original love as a human being had required it to be.

Commitment wasn't there, you only find people who don't belong, we didn't deserve as well, however, deep down inside, laid a true spirit of an individual who lives and exist with pride, yet not found or discovered by true love. So many have lived for a very long time here, and now we can discover a new purpose, with better beginnings, a different way has founded us, which will be our foundation to everlasting happiness.

This will be the new path for our lives, created for those who still longs for true love, no matter how difficult it can be to find ourselves within the context of this religion, yet we have been saved. We might not be the best that has ever happened in this beautiful creation, but we are people who matter, and we will somehow strive to make a difference into the lives of human beings and everyone that we come across. All we needed was to be shown the way, to be forgiven, not to be abandoned by love and life, we only wanted to be content of who we are, and to have our purpose realized for what it is.

Maybe there's more to creating a loving foundation, given that whether is within a formal way or not, if you can go back to that person that you love, hold him or her still in your arms, the whole world disappears. True love becomes the only reality that exists, regardless of the fact that we could have been guilty or not, now there's only one truth that is real between us. It might not be a package meant for our whole lives, however, if you can hold on tight to it, is something that you can live through for the rest of your life.

At the end, all these ways that we feel are best for what we need, or what we are, only applies to when we are separated from each other. How to motivate the other to move where they are, from one place to another, just to come, meet and be with that specific person whom you love.

As distance can separate human being's from loving one another truly, and discipline, like a religion as known to be, is there to strengthen the bond with that special being, that you long to be with, against the other partner's absence. To have faith in the communion that we serve as a unity, that you are not gone too far or forever, and that you will come back to honor the true love we share together.

That's where we are or find ourselves stuck in today's world, we want to be reunited with the people that we love the most, without having to pretend like we can cope with the situation. Given that modernization can come in between lovers, and has been introduced against everything that we are, and when life has become this modern thing that we didn't expect it to be, how do you remain content? As we have young families, you want to start your own family as well, and you want discipline installed in that household, so that you're sure that even if you're not around, you know your partner is safe.

There are three types of households; in the old tradition, you and your wife live with your family, and you the male go far to work there permanently, and return home once in a while. In the modern lifestyle, you have your own household separately, you both live together and labor where you are, and you leave in the morning and come back in the afternoon.

The last ones are business orientated families, where both of you stay at home, you don't work, you live together with each other every day. However, to be part of these lifestyles, you need to be blessed as love can be held back, if you are not within a discipline that thoroughly looks into the well-being of everything that you doing, given that all of this is cycled within a loving condition.

Trust has another big role to play in this lifestyles, if you can look carefully we have only allowed ourselves to be far or responsible for loving someone when you know that they are safe, and they are not doing anything against the union you have with each other. If not people are not worthy of being trusted or is just the way love goes, you have to be within a cycle that focuses and deeply concentrates on how true love is shared among individuals, or just to be in a reasonable condition of faith.

We pray for modern families to be our heritage as you're able to start your own family, work where you are, and share in the beauty of love every day and be happy with your lives. That is how true love is supposed to create happiness in our day to day basis. More than that you have all this as something that though it seems so easy, yet it isn't, it could become one of the most difficult thing you can ever achieve. You want to live well knowing that we have been given these platforms to be human and that when an opportunity to commit has come, you will be blessed with one of the three households that will allow you to be within a loving union.

You want to be sure that nothing can stand against anything that you choose to be part of. For I have never known my reason for studying beyond, however, I am certain that of all that there is, I deserve to be among one of the families, of living happy with your partner every day, or working right where you are. So this are some of the things that belong to true love, you can never have it all given without an entity that looks after your well-being, even the old traditional household can be very difficult to achieve at times.

At this point, you have to understand that when human beings had been suffering from lacking discipline. All kinds of bad things had come into their world, and they couldn't find an opportunity to come back from being forsaken by life. Now we have reached a place of love where we belong and believe our desires are rightly taken care of, because when you need a relationship, you want something that has meaning, and is meant for you to be happy.

Given that you can be able to understand that our lives becomes something very disappointing when there's no true love, as so much can be held back against everything that you need. When a relationship becomes worthy for human beings to be together, it has benefits for both couples to enjoy, and it's a package of life, and of the love that they will grow old with.

When there's no room for love within your heart, you look for someone with the right qualities to be with everywhere in the world, yet there's none, you try to find the simplest meaning, still nothing makes sense. Whereas it has been the area where we needed to grow, to see ourselves working everything out and finding a purpose in what we are.

Mostly what hurt the most is that we couldn't be anything that we desired, and at the same time be in a relationship where we're truly devoted. More like we couldn't be what we truly cared about, whatever there could've been, wasn't healthy for everyone, I guess at the end we want the true love with the life that we have chosen for ourselves.

Sikhs is a discipline that deals with the morality of love, how to maintain trust and remain motivated, especially in the path of education, and not to ever forsake who we are. It creates a plea that human beings are very important regardless of what they have done or become. Even when they have already engaged in things that are not seen appropriate, is not the end of their world. They could have failed to realize what life required from them at first, however, is not the conclusion of their worth, they still deserve a second chance.

Unlike in Christian discipline where man and woman must follow the traditional route of marriage before engaging in bodily activities. Once they engage in the acts of relationships not yet committed, then Christianity will fail to protect them from everything out there, work, life, love, and happiness.

Chapter Six

The exchange of life

When you are with someone every day, you live together and share so much with each other, that you don't even remember who's dependent on the other. Yet a man is supposed to be the one that takes the lead on supporting a woman, however, it is not always the monetary part that creates dependency.

There could be a need for emotional support, the essence of our lives in loving each other, the exchange of life that love must have on individuals. What do we give within our relationships as people that is so special about one another, that we can never have an opportunity to share with someone else, what is the most essential thing that you offer to the other?

Sharing is one thing that you must have true value for within a loving situation, given that as human beings we coming from different backgrounds. Our experiences are not the same, they differ so much, and somewhere so deep, the roots we have are formed by unique beliefs. My experience has been that of living without love, of being alone, isolated, of having the whole world concerned about what is it that I engage in, how I act on things and when do I think of love and acting upon such a feeling.

So when I come into a relationship I feel so saddened by my experience, and from where I come from a human being that feels the same way about you is hard to come across, you can search all around only to find that there is none.

What do you bring into each other's lives that you're prepared to share as man and woman that could have realized how important love is? I have brought this amazing feeling of caring, and understanding that what you giving me, is what a lot could have failed to give. Being my partner comes with knowing that you came out of so many people to take the role that they couldn't play in my life, and that is what makes every human being special for who they are. Someone must always be enough for you, given the circumstances that you have chosen to be with that person from among so many.

Is never something that you can grasp easily, how valuable and meaningful someone's love or presence is, given the opportunity that I will live the rest of my life with a person that I admire so much. I had no quality education as a young man, my knowledge became that of learning how to understand everything on my own. As I was studying for a very long time I became aware that so much that I wanted, is now officially based on the idea that I must figure out things for myself.

I had to master everything that I had known to be very important in life, including the love for someone, it wasn't something that I could find just like that. I could have completed my whole youth searching for true love, never did I meet anyone to commit to or became a parent. I found myself stuck, wondering about knowledge and what I wanted, what came to my mind for me to understand is that, you could have known things. Only to learn that you will have everything that you desire, including your partner, family, as well as money, but as for your lover, is the only one who became the person that they're among so many out there.

I know that it could have been anyone, yet in the end, the universe only allowed for that one special person to come into my life, and then you ask yourself, how important is this human being, and what makes him or her unique from all the people that I have ever known, how valuable is this unique being?

The part where you must be able to say that, I haven't had an opportunity to love and be loved, I have shared every day alone, and yet longing for someone to give myself to. I never had that particular individual who understands and cares about me, and now that I have met a person like that, I should rejoice, resemble true love, and celebrate the joy which that has brought into my daily well-being.

Bring happiness into someone's life, as much as they have brought joy into yours, what I wanted never existed for a very long time. Then there was the world that took me by surprise and showed me that I could wish for things, yet is the kind that you can never have easily. You cannot trust anything or anyone, there is nothing to have easy, and I'm coming from all these kinds of experiences into a relationship that I hadn't known when it would arrive. Even if I knew, however it was with this specific person that it came into existence, out of millions of human beings.

You are someone coming from exercising your beliefs, deep inside you have felt how difficult the world can be, that you can't even smile any more, as so much has been against the person that you are. You have a lot that you wanted to achieve, so far you haven't achieved anything, even your heart has weaken because you've allowed love to pass you. You were almost convinced that you have reached your destination only that you haven't arrived and having to live with that.

You know that loving someone is not something that happens every day, but once in a lifetime you can meet a person fully prepared to love you, the way you are, and having to put up with so much of you. Today when I look at you, the one who has become my perfect choice, whom I spend every day with, I can hardly believe anything. I know you didn't come so easy, at some point in my life I had lost faith in relationships, yet you came just to show me how important I am, and that is true love you have for me.

So much along the way was not how you wanted things to be, and you felt very disappointed, life had been very challenging, and when you finally got to a point of understanding. You were extremely tired because situations had been very stressful, and love as well was not the simplest thing to have, especially in conditions like this. So now that you have find someone who loves you, ask yourself, how many have failed before you reached at this one, who gave you the world?

Everything there is or what matters the most in a relationship is sharing the truth, love, and honesty. You exchange yourselves to each other, by continuously giving to one another who you are, you bond deep within. Even your gestures at times can be very similar, and not to mention that at a particular point we become one.

We can resemble the same thing, or maybe come together in our kids, when you look at this new life you realize that both of us became united. We have so much to offer to one another, you only need to make sure that is good you offering to the other. Now that you've offered so much of who you are, when you have completely given all that, what is there left to give to someone else.

You know when you have been heartbroken, and you tried by all means necessary to forget. You are coming from a situation like that, which had been very difficult to pass through, everything was always against the person that you are, whatever you try to achieve, becomes impossible. Then you needed to be patient, to understand things clearly and learning how to move forward with life.

Although our lives can be robbed by situations we encounter along the way, you must try to make something out of it, by becoming strong in those conditions that you know are not comfortable for you to pass through. In order to find a path that moves forward, you have to learn to put things behind, and think of it rather as a learning curve, a challenge that wouldn't be easy to thrive through.

At times losing your partner can lead to a very heart-breaking situation, and everything that you are just become imprisoned from that. Although people as well can do so much to influence true love and relationships, which can make you lose focus on healing your soul, we tend to forget how to love again.

You become so weak in ever committing to loving a person, at times I wanted to cry, because of how I felt separated from everything that is meaningful, through that one incident. My whole life seemed to flow on the direction of living without anything that matters, you are never given enough chance to work through your heart, before you know, so much has interfered and time has left you behind.

From just a small setback, you find yourself struggling with coming back to being a human that matters, you feel so pushed and needing to learn so much about life. Love becomes a challenge on a daily basis, because you got used to having plenty easily. Is when you have lived in a relationship where you have done a lot. That you went out of your way just to be with one another, and pleasing each other in a way that has built your happiness.

Then there was the world at large, that you had seen, live, celebrate, and enjoyed together, then one day you separate from loving each other, and you don't even try to fight for what you had. You just give up on love like that, when something of that nature has occurred, you lose yourself and you don't know where to find those pieces of your heart. The situation could be very comforting when you still want each other, and try to make things work.

Depending on how deep are the scars of your soul you can never want to be healed from a situation like that. It becomes a life lesson of knowing that you can be broken, that someone can promise true love and never deliver on their word. Is a period of learning that something bad can happen to you as well.

Somehow it was all fine the way things had happened, and then I looked back only to find that what has occurred is wrong. However, did I know I would never find who I am and what I used to be? No, that person had permanently died spiritually. To be normal I had to invent a new human being, and that person had been born differently from whom I used to be, now I was conscious of everything. I became aware of the value of something or someone, I was now living with the worth of loving truthfully and honestly.

My heart was not as weak as it used to be, it had changed and become a little stronger than it was once, however, I could only live my life on a spiritual level. Given that when you have lost someone, depending on how much you have shared, it becomes difficult for the world to accommodate both of you at the same time.

Love is strong to pass through when you have loved each other so much, you can try to know who is wrong or right, and you can take it further from that. When you want to be the correct one, you inherit that as your way of life and you keep living in that route.

As for the wrong part in the relationship continues in that path of dishonesty, the battle becomes something that you want to prove to each other, that regardless of what happened the world was always like that. When true love wasn't there from the beginning, where was I supposed to find it, you feel like your life is coming to an end. As you will have the whole universe questioning everything that you doing, and that's how one might developed this spiritual consciousness trying to save themselves from all that has gone bad.

You can never know what you have given to each other, your strength and weaknesses, or what you have learned in one another, which you cannot tolerate about the other, let alone the world being enough for the two of you. When you give yourself to someone you don't know what they might become from the way they insist on having their own will continuing to happen, and how that can seek to devour your soul. I became a very good, knowledgeable person in love and realize that you cannot live to please someone at your own expense.

When you have faith in love you can never change your purpose, you see every situation as a calling for you to understand life out there, to discover this world on your own, where it is mostly important to human lives. Is when you are curious about a lot and finding out how much something means, to take part in the creation of the universe, and create your understanding where you find it very essential.

We have our businesses and careers, then there's life and love, and you have to find the balance in all of these, business changes, new ones outplay the old, the world is hungry for fresh ideas, and modern ways on how to make things happen. So much could be influenced by that as well and adjusted to modernization, yet true love stays the same. It remains true in every way that there is, and that's how we like it, we admire that genuine part about it, because it is love when it's in that nature.

It doesn't need to be influenced by anything or anyone, it just wanted to remain true, yet in this business, of this new age that we have begun living our lives. You find that so much has been changed, tied down by machines of money and time, and love no longer true, and when you lose someone that you loved. You will be consumed by the duration of how man and woman have been moving forward with making and loving each other truly, things are now made to be recognized how important they are.

You cannot keep up with everything going on around you, when you learn to adjust in this universe, is through love for a human being. You become part of creation from the commitment you have with someone special, you remaining content of the world around you and all that lives. When you lose focus from the center of creativity, all that is meant to keep you alive disappears, now something is trying to shift your focus.

True love helps us to travel at the same pace with life, and when you are deeply committed to each other, you just move with all that creates effortlessly. Your mind is fully updated on whatever is going on. You can get left-back if you are found without anyone to commit to, how can you know so much by heart? Your head can only remember how to survive, not to excel.

You can never know what you give to someone, only the receiver can be able to notice the difference that you have brought into their life. Imagine knowing what a person is bringing into your existence, after years of searching and looking for a person that you can trust into a relationship with you, and there were never there for any reason or specific purpose.

When you try to be involved in so much that exists, love can disappear at times, as you may not be entirely strong in all areas, and that can have an effect on how you progress with life. I was working on a certain project that had changed everything that I was, and it was now rooted in my beliefs, and it had become my foundation into this world.

As bad as I was growing up and becoming a man, there was nothing that came before that, it had become the genuine belief of the life that I live, and I was right about so much living like that. I just wanted someone who can come in the knowledge that I had gained serving that purpose, a person who can understand all that I have turn out to be through this work, even if it means that we oppose or stand against a lot of ideas.

That became the only thing that I truly knew and understand, it was my world, outside I didn't exist, and knowledge can bring hope and faith. With thoroughly understanding life like I had known that, it was my only way to success, a journey I could've hoped to travel easy. However, it never turn out to be a simple idea to live by as you know the world has competition, which is part of everything that is happening, and you can be pushed to acknowledge that you not strong for now.

Yet that doesn't matter, what's important is that you were able to notice the difference between what you are and what someone is, and better because when you begin to see the variation, you start understanding where you stand. Man are a reflection of life and woman reflect love, both can respond very well by showing you where you are or where you could've failed.

When you combine the two you begin to understand where you are left back, unlike focusing on your ideas and never seeing the shift, learning to look into the change that your life represents to others helps to adjust very well to everything.

It's all out there, you know very well that you can't have something when you don't understand what it is that you doing, and most of it love. The partner that has been created by your understanding, what are you willing to do for that person? The human being that your mind has made for you, and doesn't care about anything in the world except that they embrace your ideas.

Its love that one has come to offer, and give your life a meaning, when you have given everything that you have to a particular subject, and it's all that matters more than anything. Something that can never be replaced in your heart, and someone comes in and becomes part of that.

Part Two

Part Two

Passion

The flames that burn between two people that have true love and feelings for each other, a genuine reflection of the connection that they share deep within their souls. It is something that could have been normal, however, it exceeded the level in which they were to understand. You never know what you sharing with someone when you making love, you will not be able to understand until you're completely old, alone, and unable to take part in that kind of bliss for life.

Then you begin to miss those days that you were able to do so much with pride. Loving a person is giving yourself to them when you still matter. When there's a lot you have to offer, so much to live for, enthusiasm for creation burning in your eyes.

Try to imagine in a relationship, it is where we find ourselves sharing more of who we are, than with the rest of humanity. Our world is meaningless, without the other that loves just as much as you, and from that cycle of surrender to our innermost desire. Comes the true joy about life and love that emerges from deep within our soul, the only thing that is worth celebrating about our lives.

From the hearts of people that have had an opportunity to share in the most blessed relationships, in the passion of life and love deeper than anyone has ever imagine. Comes true joy and oneness, they stand together in whatever they do, trying to resemble something that is deep in their soul. That it is within a loving cycle that they have had a chance to be completely happy and be satisfied with all that they are. So much that they never even doubted the rest of their lives, that it is everything to live for.

True love is a good story, the best part about life, and you don't want to turn that into a bad thing, yet dishonesty can change the nature of how things are. More than we care for each other, is the passion that we share, everything compared to how deep love is? What is it that it means in this world, or in our lives, to have loved a person so much with all that you have, to devote your entire being to who someone is?

How committed can we give ourselves to one another, and to everything that there is, how deep or what defines the depths of true love? The depth of love is best defined by how long two people have stayed together within a relationship, sharing every day and giving in to each other with complete devotion, and dedication to pleasing the other all the time.

Passion is when you surrender yourself to your partner by offering them your complete being, striving to satisfy and make them happy, working hard to fill that void of yearning for joy produced by the union of hearts.

You know when there's love, then there is no limit to how much of yourself you give to the other, and when you offer what you are like that. You do it with passion in spirit and physically, humbly dedicated to loving one another, withholding nothing, and without care about tomorrow. When true love has brought you together, you do not care about what the next day might bring. All that matters is here, where we are right now, the rest doesn't matter, given that if we can't make each other happy today, then there won't be any future.

The most important part of everything is that you can give the best of each other right now, where you are. Seize the greatest moment of your lives and share true love, make love, with passion, showing the other how much they mean to you, and how you care about one another.

Could it be that as people we could have failed to grasp enough knowledge about what there is to share in a relationship, or what our partners really have in mind? And what does it takes for the other to realize how deep your love is? Maybe it is just meant for one to deeply commit themselves and to suffer from everything when you not giving in completely.

Until you reach at that stage of permanent break up, and without the need to make-up and you are now through, very stressful and a confusing situation to be at. That no matter what you do your hearts will never be one again, and what now becomes the reality is to try and forget about what you had, within your souls, you know you have separated, and cannot be lovers again.

Depending on how deep you went with each other, everyone can suffer the setback, we all have so much that changes from a relationship, and you realize that you've lost more than enough from loving the other. After kids a lot has died, even when you want to commit again in the future, you can never do it from the level where you use to be, and you will live with the regret of knowing that if I had given myself to the right person, I wouldn't live my life divided like I am.

So we all have a lot to lose, the female's cry for the person she used to be, though she cannot regret where she is right now. You only blame yourself for not finding a partner that will love you the way you deserved to be loved forever.

While you're officially stuck in that old age, and no matter what you do or try, you cannot forget about each other, and from that moment that you have decided to turn against one another, you are permanently separated. You can have the remaining of what used to be, of your lives, but what had mattered between you has disappeared.

You can never be united again, all the love that once brought you together is gone, and you are now living as separate beings. Whatever comes after that is regrets and trying to cope with life, and nothing can ever make things right or be enough for you to be happy.

Love is deep serves as a reminder that relationships can be seen as an easy thing to have, or to live with or without. That in a communion you can overlook too many important things which must be taken into consideration, only to realize later how crucial that has been. So you can rather choose to learn by your own will and maybe from other people's mistakes, or you can experience life through your greatest loss or setback.

The thing is that we all know what is right, regardless of who you are, things do make sense at some point, and you can decide from there to be a better individual, who values your partner. You choose the person you are for yourself, not from coming into contact with someone, like that life would have been very easy. Even if you find something that is real, you can lose focus when you haven't made up your mind, about being committed permanently.

You must choose to be discipline in loving one another, if you don't want to experience the difficulties of relationships, knowing very well that everything could impact back to who you are. You stop and ask yourself, who am I, and why do I need to value this person that I am? Given that you know situations won't make it easy for you to be certain of what you doing if you haven't decided, how you must live your life.

If you are to avoid hardships along the way, then try to get things right the first time, don't learn by mistakes, even if it means that you have to order yourself on a general level. It could be what you require to understand things better, as so much that matters seems to be influenced by the same thing, love, life, all complements one another.

Why do we separate with those we have loved the most, is it how we fail to give ourselves to each other because of what we commit ourselves to? What are the capabilities that we possess towards loving one another, can there be a very good way in which we can explain what attaches human beings? Does true love exists, or is just people learning to live together, and settling for whatever there is? If there's anything like love out there, then what are the grounds for commitment, do we give our hearts, and leave a space for disappointment in the future?

So that you can get out of the relationship, or find it easy for you to move on with life, when what you had is no longer there, and if we think that there won't always be love, then how do we prepare our lives for it? Commitment is what we must constantly ask ourselves of, exactly what is it that you can get out of giving in, or loving someone completely? Or is it that we must live everyday being aware that if things are to go wrong, so much can become difficult to cope with?

I searched for love in every direction, and couldn't find anyone to be with, and what makes it worse when you reach the end, is that for most of your life that opportunity was always there and you didn't care. Now you need someone who can give in and commit to you forever, from the bottom of each other's hearts, and that human being is nowhere to be found. Again knowing that you require this person to give something so strong and definite, it is all that matters, and if you cannot have an individual like that you will never be happy.

The reason for understanding this is to elaborate how valuable being committed to loving your partner is, as part of everyone's life. So that we can find the real worth when love is still there, and not to acknowledge after it has passed how it required one to consider the other very seriously. Maybe we cannot know if a relationship is really true or not, however, it feels as if something is watching over all that we do, or refuses for human beings not to be honest in that area. To succeed it needs someone to understand how deep are the bonds that we develop as we continue being together on a daily basis, and not to compromise meaning by thinking less of what your lover truly means.

I found myself lost, and looking for answers to what it means, the real meaning behind life's most important concept, love. As I couldn't come back, from one of my mid-life's biggest disappointments, it happened once, and my heart was permanently broken, and surely I could convince myself that what we had was not true love. There were things that we knew going into this relationship were not based in honesty or there to call it a communion, however, at the end of the day when something goes wrong, you find yourself stuck.

We can say that we had quality time, and best moments together, and most of it was unforgettable. Yet all of this was built on top of a lie or no real commitment, and that it couldn't at the end be worth cherishing, or meant to last forever. It wasn't easy to get to that point where we trust each other, because of how we begun, what have I lost from such an encounter of life? To have met someone accidentally, and share a wonder of love that could never set anyone free. We both didn't matter to one another, but why can't we just move on with our lives, or find a new place to begin, what went wrong?

I didn't know what I have done so badly, as things have never been impossible to handle like they have turn out to be this time. I had no idea of what was missing, somehow I realized I could've lost my purpose to love, by living a lie, and to find how happy I used to be, I would have to fix it, and that to once again be joyful is depended on me and what I need to understand. I had searched for myself in every corner of the world, and for a very long period, yet I still couldn't be content of who I am.

Now I was desperate, and wanted to know the cause of everything I'm going through, and that is not happening to me since maybe I have sinned. I needed a new beginning more than anyone can ever imagine, I had begun to feel as if everyone is out to get me. Though I could try to defend myself, but I wasn't winning, given that regardless of who you are, we are not always right about everything. You begin to realize that perhaps there could be something you didn't do well along the way.

You cannot look for true love, and not find a solution, a good partner must be easy to attract, if someone worthy isn't simply to have, then so much could be wrong with your life. So now that I have aged, I began to understand, that maybe we are not always correct about everything, especially when you have reached a stage where relationships must begin to make sense. You may be remaining behind from something that you could have done, or it might be anything that you failed to do right, and now you need to look into it.

Again could there be underlying issues like cultures, ethnic, and all other type of staff, love has to keep from human beings, where things are not difficult to maintain? Where within these cycles of existence, there is something worth sharing? And for most of your life you have been traveling in the wrong side of things, where almost everything that you desire is just a struggle.

Does the differences that we resemble as part of our ethnic, lifestyle, or cultural background has anything to do with how we feel about each other? Do we find it comfortable within a certain culture, or ethnicity that we can rather remain within that cycle of life, than to share ourselves with other human beings, or maybe with the rest of the world? Is when you look for answers, and you don't know where to find them, as it seems to be hard finding the right person.

What went wrong between us, could we have exchanged something so special, and that we have never shared with anyone else? Maybe my life or yours would have been better, as we got stuck there. Could those moments still form part of our greatest memory, if it does, then how do we pass such a great memorable period in our lives?

Maybe I failed to realize the quality of the time we've spent together, makes more sense than anything, to have experienced something that deep down inside you cannot forget, or be able to pass through. Honesty and confrontation, what experiences this kind of excitement in us, which cannot be fooled, or settle for anything less? And how do you accept, or acknowledge that and be able to move on with your life.

I needed to know the answers to such a trauma, could it be that again we must learn to respect life and its properties of creation? Nothing is less significant. Everything that we do deserves quality attention, it's not something that could have been done somehow, although you may not have committed, it is all that exist between two people in a relationship.

I needed so much answered, so that I can be sure of where I am, and what I need to do, and be able to alter my attitude towards committing to a human being. Given that regardless of whether we accept it or not, change does heal some part in every person. To try something new and with dedication, even if it's not usual, but with all the willingness and determination that one has to love, maybe you can experience new wonders of life that might lead to happiness.

Maybe found something that could bring my focus back to true love, given that overtime one's attention could change, from being a loving person, to caring about something else. Such as money, or a career which is difficult to accomplish overnight, or whatever it could be other than giving in to a person. So how do I come back to committing myself to that special being once more?

Will my intentions to love truly and be trustworthy in this new age deliver me? If that is not enough what could stand in my way, in that path that leads to everlasting happiness, as you understand that you can never be young again. With all my powers to commit honestly focused in the right direction, that once brought us together, be adequate for me to experience new love, and without the need to be judged? Although it was not perfect, it has interrupted our lives, from focus to being unfocused. What did meeting with a certain man or a woman had on you, which you can never have with anyone?

Now life has become much worse than it was before, and what's the change that I could have experienced without realization? I was looking for a way in which I can find true love again, but I couldn't arrive there, let love take me back. One might think that it meant the same as before, while it means something different, this time is real, and from within the center of my heart.

What is passion, how do you define being passionate? I am not talking about the enthusiasm for one thing and failing the other. The thrill of life and love that drives you towards, to want more out of everything and true love. Something that seeks to experience the best out of all of existence, even though there can be mistakes, but rectifying them by a way of leaning on the truth, as you seek quality out of all that lives.

You might not know what had happened over the years, and you could have gone through the same experience over and again, and as painful as it has been. You must understand that it doesn't matter where you are, you need to start exercising caring about a person, and deepening your focus on it. Life is in spirit and true love is in physical form, you can withhold your ideas about your understanding for someone to see what you thinking or value, yet love must show, be able to resemble how much you care.

As you deepen your focus on life's most important concepts, you feel the need to love truly, you begin to acknowledge that is impossible to be happy without anyone who cares about you. Along the way to witness yourself moving towards a better direction, you have to find out exactly what matters, and how to dedicate your entire being to it. For as long as I have lived, I've been trying to understand so much, to discover a way to create meaning out of everything. Though situations can be very confusing, somehow I did comprehend that all of it makes no sense, without a good partner who shares the same interest with you.

One can spend almost every day trying to say too much of everything, yet all that will ever come out of it is to say that. How do you know when you have loved someone so deep, or that you have given a lot of who you are? And the fact that you can never be able to do anything without that special person who was once there, and you allowed to pass. At the end how do we value our lives enough, to accept that we didn't realize at first that loving or having a good partner has been the best gift, and the source of our happiness.

As if here in this current existence we are only meant to love one person, and this human being is the only individual who you supposed to give all your life to, and with giving there is no limit to how much of ourselves we offer to each other. You just have to surrender what you are, or everything you have ever known, after that there is nothing remaining for you to live for, accept for that only being.

It happens that we are not supposed to ever live each other for the rest of our lives, yet this world created by God, and ruined by human beings. It knows when you have given enough of everything that you are to what you care about, or to each other. It comes and ruin all that you value, withholding lovers from loving one another, for love that didn't come so easy.

This is how we have had our lives ruined, in relationships we have been wronged, from all that has happened you can realize how important, and limited an opportunity to love and be loved by a human being has been. Now that you have separated with the only one you have ever cared for, you cannot find anyone to be there for you again.

To which level of commitment do we need to have given ourselves to one another, for us to feel that we can no longer go back, to loving anyone again? And who has denied us the opportunity to see, or realize before we can understand that love is very important, and a precious possession to value. If it is modernization that has changed what we knew, it was the strangest towards combining human beings and connecting hearts.

Can we start all over again? As what we had has been interrupted, and we cannot love each other the way we use to, something has come in between our lives. Now we are no longer capable of loving the way it must be done, we can try but our chances have been ruined. Maybe you can ask for someone who has a heart that loves to forgive you, to accept you back to life, given that only a human being capable of true love, and forgiving can be able to heal you back to being normal once more.

Chapter Seven

Center of life

My world had been darkened by situations that I had gone through, I somehow felt lost and detached from all that matters, yet it didn't discourage or push me to have been lazy. I motivated myself to establish my own understanding, I discovered so much where I was focused, and the outcome of that has been truly amazing. Although time can get the best of you, from how long it can take to find the true purpose to all that creativity means, and the fact that when you engage in whatever you find necessary.

At times you can keep going around in circles, without realizing that it is within the center of who we are where you need to focus your attention. To be able to find answers that are relevant to all that life means, the real meaning to our innermost desire, and the results of what love must produce for a human being.

It was long after I abandoned myself where I had been committed to someone, that I became aware something unusual has happened to me, I felt empty, deserted, and alone. It became impossible for true love to ever be real again, what happened to the person that I am, one who was loved and admired deeply? How would you know what you have done, to bring this kind of loneliness into your life? Is when we lose focus on love, that our lives begins to stray away from all that matters, and from the center of what controls our entire understanding.

You find yourself traveling in a path that has no meaning, you begin to disappear where life unfolds, where we draw knowledge to understand who we are. However, when love is the central focus in our hearts, everything begins to make sense, and create a meaningful impact, in every part of our entire being. Love dwells at the center of our lives, and our inner self, deep down within our soul, and listens to all that we desire most.

It doesn't compete with anything, or anyone, moves along with all that creates, and that should be for every man and woman. If you avoid leaving it behind, then you will never struggle for whatever you yearn for. Except that you will reach everything and the only person who you longed to be with, someone who cares about you, and your ambitions.

There's always a special being for everyone out there, and when you meet that human being, you must hold on tight, and give in to them with your whole heart, don't deny yourself an opportunity to be happy in a relationship. True love is the cornerstone for all our needs, the source of our happiness, the pillar of our lives, and whatever it is that we require in our entire existence.

If there was a rule that governs how we give ourselves to each other, then we would have known how to commit to one another better. We would've been made aware that if I ever lose this person that life has blessed me with, then I will never find another who will care for me this much. So since we lack knowledge in loving our partners truly, we are found abandoning our loved ones, the only people who have ever cared for us.

What if the love that we give to each other is not supposed to be separated, or just to be taken away from someone that cares about you. What we are to one another becomes a tool very vital to a human being's progress. Something that heals a special part in our lives, a great achievement that you've received, and now you will be heading to the next level of your life goals. What if I lose focus here at the center of creation because you took your heart away from me?

A lot of those who became aware of the essence of who they are early, have found themselves living their best lives here at the center, where true love is the central concept. It is the kind of life that is focused on caring about that special individual, it exists and beats for one human being only. It is of the nature that remains together, and shares so much with one another, and emphasizes on the bonds of the body, mind, and spirit. When you get closer to creation, you begin to realize that it is the only thing that creates happiness, and understanding in relationships and families.

For you to arrive at this level, you need to let go of everything that exists out there, and focus on what you desire most, here it is caring for a human being that matters. If you ever find that person who will give you that nature of acceptance, your life becomes an ever flowing abundance of happiness.

As much as there's joy to be found in this kind of giving to what love is, what if someone disappoints you here at the center of all that you are, and you cannot help yourself? Given that it is the only thing that lives which is true about who we are, and you become completely broken, and you feel powerless to rise back again.

It is something that you might consider very seriously when you learn to value concepts, when your mind becomes occupied since you have chosen to participate in the creativity, or creation of the world. When a lot of things have come into being, and you start focusing on different kind of situations, world theories, and the depth of everything thereof.

When there are important things to deal with, and you automatically become a subject to the Masters of life, and of the spiritual world. You see a lot coming to pass, things you should have been doing, yet, even if you want to, there's just that hold. Something is stopping you, from finding your true power, your connection with all of existence, it is no longer easy to find time to dedicate to love, there's just too much fighting a human being.

You could have seen so many who died here at the center, from whatever could have produced that kind of outcome. You disappear where you are a human being that had known who you are, how to care, or feel for everything and that someone special.

Like you have been pulled back from everything that creates, and from being involved with true love, a human being mustn't remain with facing the world through their mentality. Love complements our lives, it completes all that we are, when it has been pulled back, taken away from your entire being. You become detached, you're no longer involved with life, you die at the center, as it is evident that to just be alive alone is not enough to make you a progressive person.

I could have not understood what happened at first, and maybe I didn't care, I thought that it was just a normal thing to have gone through. It was after years when I got to realize that there's something missing, you begin to see that you are no longer part of all that creates. You are not where you must be, and you might need to look at how you got left back in so much, including relationships as well, how you have lost your true purpose on everything that matters, When love is in your heart, you feel alive, you can never compete with anyone for anything, you are just where you're required to be, and completely relevant to whatever is going on.

When you are involved with loving someone deeply, the more you exchange your love with one another, the deeper you descend and becoming part of everything together. Every day you keep descending until you pass everyone that had formed part of the cycle of your life, including family and very close friends. As you focus on giving in to each other, it is the further you keep passing all the bonds that had created who you are. And of whatever it is that exists when one hasn't find love for someone, into the center of your inner person, where you reach the worth of a good relationship, and true love for the union that you share.

When you become separated from the one you have traveled through the joy of your hearts like that, you are now divided from everything that had formed part of your cycle of love. Including whatever it is that you truly cared for, and you were all here, gathered at the center of life, family, friends, and your loved one as well, you had come together, to meet and celebrate the only gift of what lives.

When you are abandoned by that nature of love, your spirit begins to suffuse the world from how you had been committed, especially letting go of loving someone, mostly one you truly cherished. You become alone, isolated, and vulnerable to situations, then at a later stage you are surprised at the wonder of what has walked away from your life. Is only when you start searching for yourself that you can begin to realize the impact of what has left your center, as you do soul confrontation, trying to find what has deserted you. From how the loss of true love has torn your inner being apart, of which you will find what you are, if you can strive to pick up the pieces of your heart with faith.

The kind of faith that becomes the ultimate key in caring oneself, which has the power to rebuild all that has been lost in love and commitment, only that you're no longer where, or what you use to be. Your focus has strayed away from where you had been committed to loving someone, you became a human being somewhere else, but not formed by true love. You can now admire a new part of yourself, which is about you, and your ambitions, no family, friends, or loved ones.

It becomes difficult to ever find the connection back to life, with everyone that you ever cared for, especially family, and friends. While to have normal progress once more you might need to reconnect with them again, as they're not the ones to blame for your loss. If you don't ever achieve those bonds the way it used to be, is like you blaming them for your heartbreak and loneliness.

It is our first heart that suffers the loss, the one we are born with, which carries with it a lot of memories and innocence from childhood. Which is how we became bonded with everyone that had formed part of our inner cycle or that of love. Our hearts at the center of life formed by the experience of this world never breaks, it keeps growing stronger in the search for true love, and strives to create pleasure and happiness as you go along. It refuses to go back, however, continues to nurture the experiences we have had, even if you go through other difficulties, it never affects anyone closer to you and what you care for.

We all have so much that we care for, and we can at times stop realizing how important someone is, from the time we need to devote to our ambitions. And there's a lot that could trigger that, it could be a little misunderstanding that occurred which could have been resolved, and you somehow decided to take everything emotionally. Whereas the situation didn't require for anyone to get angry, you just needed to avoid that minor incident. So that you can protect what you have which is highly valued, your relationship, of which is the most precious from whatever it is that you have or can achieve.

Love is pure, when you seek to commit yourself to it, do it with good intentions at heart, as that kind of devotion sees through everything that we give ourselves to. Be honest to your partner regardless of what the past could've done to you. See no other way available for you to become a human being, have that undying faith, patience, and forgive in a way that allows you to be a human again. Though some things can easily be put behind, while with others you can't, and when one has wronged you in a way that cannot be forgiven, then you have won. True love will punish that particular individual forever, and you win the battle from within.

There's no one who is meant to be a victim or just to be vulnerable to love, we all can get hurt, learn to value something when you have it. Do not ruin your life or hurt someone else, thinking that no one will ever know or see what has happened. You are not only failing yourself in relationships, but you ruining your entire well-being, even when some things could've been coming to an end. It can continue to have you lingering there, in those impossible situations, that you want to see disappear.

There's always a situation which you can't put behind, whenever you think that is over, it comes back to haunt you. Even when you met someone that you hope is true love, only to discover that the person is not completely into commitment. It could be anything that you've been struggling with for a very long time, and it refuses to go away. Whether it be life or relationships, it can never be what you hoped for, is just not where you want to be, there is no real care or love there, and you cannot break out of that nature of circumstances.

You only get what you give, and if you haven't worked to accumulate abundance of love for someone, a human being, then you have nothing to offer. While you constantly ask yourself, why am I alone? Or why haven't I met a special person, whom I can cherish, trust, and give all that I am to? What makes us realize, that what we feeling is loneliness? Is it because we lack an individual that we can value truly and with deeper commitment in our lives?

Love at the center is about value, and sharing, we share who we are to each other, we bring something that the other doesn't have, and we learn to appreciate the differences. It is here where we are born new into the world, at the gateway to which true love for life, comes into being. It is where we celebrate the true gift of humanity, of masculine and feminine, then everything that we are begins to make sense.

Happiness and excitement of the body comes to life when we give to each other with commitment and honesty, and if you have not reached at this level, you haven't shared what you truly are with anyone. You have not yet arrived at the point of love and surrender to our deepest desire, whatever you have is not valued by our hearts or inner-self. True love is knowing that your partner is very important, special and unique, and his or her presence can never be repeated, and learning to treasure that.

True love is when your mind has settled in understanding everything there is about giving yourself to someone, to live and make love here where your entire being is cycled. You give all that you are, the longer you stay here, together, the stronger the bond you create with one another. You become the center for the other to live freely, to dwell easily, and breath the spirit of everlasting happiness, so much is shared, beyond what you can physically give to each other.

Love is unquestionable when you share it knowing the value of the other, you can never be bored of that special being, no matter how they give themselves to you, as you know their worth thereof.

As people we at times make mistakes that can later come and change our entire lives, or affect our relationships as well, so bad that things might never be the same again. Some can acknowledge their errors, while others would rather stand strong against everything. Even if they have to change the world, just to have the love that they need, and they refuse to settle for anything because of their past misunderstandings.

You know that you're guilty of a certain crime, but would you rather die without the most important thing in your life? No; and what do we do? We force our way until everything changes all over, even if it would take a very long time.

You find yourself in a situation where you acknowledge that you cannot undo what you have done, and everything is permanent, but you still want to live. You continue to carry that ultimate value in life, then you force your way until you begin to pull human beings that are not decisive in their own lives, into the center of your understanding. That is how you find people in places where you know they don't belong.

Sometimes we are caught off guard by situations which could be natural, while some could've been created by human beings who have seen an opportunity to take advantage of others. Mostly who are not fully decisive of their lives and what they truly desire, these are the kind of circumstances that could turn out to be very harmful to who we are. You can lose your life into something that you didn't choose for yourself, to be found lost forever and living in vain.

What are the odds that you want to see changed? Love can invite you just to challenge everything with you, side by side. You know something no human being has ever known, you have the right purpose, don't say it's love for humanity or someone when it is all self-centered.

If it's a worthy cause, and you have the right objective, then no one can stand before you and your destiny. Sometimes love gives us the strength to go on, because it is what we seek, or truly want to achieve. However, don't walk away from the good that you have as you are eager to start something new, it could be anything that is motivated by power or money. You can get there, yet you might never find yourself again, where relationships are honest, true love was there, commitment, and everything that you desired, you walked away from it.

There may not be a turning point, and maybe you can achieve your goals of power and money, only that love might refuse to ever look at you again. You walked away from yourself, from what was real, you can try only that you can never find a replacement. Rather that if you have something to achieve, is better doing it with the one that you care for, even if it brings tension, it is nothing that being committed to each other cannot solve, true love will work out the solution to everything that is happening in your lives.

Make your relationship the only purpose you have, nothing else, even when there are things that you want or maybe can't reach them, it shouldn't be what you look away from. Continue with it, and at the end, you will win, with it in your heart, and it would have conquered everything in your daily life. Whatever you do can produce what you are on the inside, or what you desire most, is only in love where our concept are centralized and seen exactly what they stand for.

Human beings must learn to stand strong for what they believe in, before they can ruin the original cause of the lives they live. You must love with everything that you have, so that you can realize your purpose to succeed come to reality.

Love will push all that you desire into the world, no matter how long it takes for human beings to realize, the aim, and objectives of everything that you lived for. I wanted my purpose to be clear, and I made sure that I haven't ruined the center, so that the seed can be of true love, I remained faithful, with, or without anyone to commit to, and it became my home.

To whatever that we do, true love is the only thing that is very relevant, and mostly to so much that we work for, which we want to achieve. A lot of these objectives they seem to be our point of focus, however, they are not the outcome, the result of what we engage in becomes love, it is always open and free for human beings to dwell in. All of it, the power and the money that motivates what we do, everything becomes something that isn't there. It might even want to change who we are, yet that tender of our hearts just becomes the simplest solution to what we desire.

So much that we work for is not what we get at the end, life defies the knowledge we have of the world, and you ask yourself, where is it, all of it that I've worked hard for? Yet, love you will find, nurtures the knowledge and the belief, it becomes the answer and the center to our innermost desires.

Chapter Eight

Flow of life

Life is formed by countless human beings, living effortlessly, you cannot deny people their worth, they mean so much to this beautiful creation, and they matter more than you think. Whatever you have been busy with, is nothing compared to moving along with all that forms this magnificent planet. When you decide to stop caring or focusing on loving your partner, you lose focus on being part of this world, love is traveling at the same pace with all that creates.

You don't stop loving your partner, no matter what you seek to achieve, find it in you to be always courageous towards caring for your loved one. The path of being in a relationship makes things easy on a human being, especially for the masculine, a man lives in his own universe. His world has a lot of divisions and separations from other male creations, yes within a cycle of love you wouldn't fail to understand things the way they are. Given that woman have forgiven everything that exists out there, they don't ask for so much, they move along with whatever forms this reality.

People are always involved in making love night and day, and traveling within the flow of life, when in a communion you have begun to criticize the quality of your lover's dedication for your union. Your relationship and trust for each other begins to slow down, and your hearts stops beating for one another, you mustn't stop or pause your devotion towards your partner. Give all that you have in your heart so that the other is always satisfied with your commitment.

The thing that will haunt you the most when you're outside a relationship, is that deep inside you know you will not live the rest of your life alone. You have that undying desire for love, you need to come back to be with someone, sooner or later you will wear out, your body, mind, and soul will begin to dehydrate, and you will want to be rejuvenated. You can try to make peace with living in isolation, yet you can't, or convince yourself by creating an agreement with your heart that is fine to be single, but is not.

You cannot solve the issue or the state of being alone, the situation becomes something that feels like you fighting a human being. Whereas this person has countless tricks to keep attacking you, and is just people continuing with caring for each other every day.

To be always loving and giving to each other all that we are, and not holding back on anything. If you ever look away, it can become very difficult for one to once again understand the language of love. You can be subjected or discriminated on ever finding someone who truly loves you, who will be willing to give you everything that they are. A person to value, and get comfortable on being in a relationship with you.

It doesn't have to stop, or pause, you must continue with giving that quality of our inner being to one another every day. True love comes from deep within our soul, yet it can never be true forever, for it to remain strong, you must nurture it with genuine understanding. So that you can find the quality in loving someone, caring for the other early, and be able to discover the real purpose in being with each other. You mustn't realize after it has passed, that to surrender yourself to your lover had been something truly meaningful.

Do not shy away on this precious gift of life, commit to one another wholeheartedly. Right from the very beginning, you must just learn to care, when you are still worthy of giving with real passion. Seize that opportunity soon in your quest for fulfillment, as you might look back and regret the chances you had of achieving true and everlasting happiness.

Relationships are good at their natural state, unlike having to come back spiritually trying to amend things. When you are at your origin is where everything is easy, unlike coming from the cold, being broken, and forsaken, thinking that someone will just take you back with open arms. That is something that can be too difficult to become a reality, like you are making special demands for human beings to be sacrificed for you to be a valid person again.

Being in a relationship is like traveling in a fast-moving train on its track, you don't jump out, you might get injured, and you stay there, and remain still, so that you don't harm yourself. Through our hearts committed to each other we are always accelerating with creation, and journeying together as one, living and loving all that life has given to us.

You could've lost someone that you truly cared for, yet it doesn't mean that you must give up, it just happened. You keep moving with the flow of life, and love will find you along the way, even if it takes a longer period. As the outcome of the situation you might find yourself in could be different, from when you have forsaken your partner, or when the other stops loving you, by not realizing that you need to value being in a relationship. So make good out of it, don't be the one who was not willing to give what they are in a communion-ship.

There is no need at all to stop and watch human beings move on with life, and loving one another, you can lie to yourself, thinking that so much isn't moving forward. They are physically and spiritually traveling with creation and creating the world, and love doesn't look back, it keeps on disappearing. Once you're left behind, you don't have to be worked out on how to catch up on things, you can call a lot of bad luck on your entire being.

What was missing, when the world had answered all your prayers, did it feel like everything became so simple, or has it turned to be more difficult now that you have subjected yourself with it? If you have failed to be true to life, you will feel like everything has seasons, as nothing is ever guaranteed. There would be times where you have to acknowledge being alone, until you find someone to love again.

Like a river to the sea, life flows in the direction of love, you don't have to wander in vain searching for something that you had, which you could've treasured, and now you don't know where to find it. Seek for happiness and answers to your deepest desire in the path of loving a human being. Even if you could've been stuck in situations that you don't know how to come out of, do not turn your back on true love.

Take it with you, struggle with it, for you to have it, without anyone understanding why you keep something viewed unnecessary. Always remember that now we have reached a certain stage where only relationships will become a difficulty to figure out, a lot of things would have come to pass.

Man and woman shall not be struggling with the means to survive, but the need to be committed to one another truthfully, that would be the secret hidden from human. How to derive satisfaction from life, and loving each other, love lives, gives, builds, and moves forward towards better creation, and everlasting happiness. At times I wondered how much a person has to give, and I could devote everything that I am, and it would make sense. On the other hand, being confident and not to be worried knowing that all we give from deep within our hearts can bring a person back from the dead.

You can act like you don't care about it, you can become ignorant for some time, but what if you know the truth, about life, and love as well. That it takes time to rebuild all that could've been lost while loving someone, true love that gives, that one needs to be happy. Then you don't need to look away, or postpone your responsibilities, show that you care right now.

The relationships we have with our loved ones, are the only thing that connects us back to reality. Even if situations don't allow you to be involved with anyone, strive to find a way back to someone's arms, before you ruin the center of your entire being, or get used to living alone forever.

It's easy to stop loving a person, yet it is hard to find someone who can replace that human being deep within your soul. The thing is that we don't know where true love came from, and we're still not sure where it disappears to, however, we all know how to begin peacefully, regardless of where we come from. I don't know why I ended up reflecting on love, only that it has been something which I know that from the depth of my heart needed sharing, talking about, and understanding why in this new age we must be alert.

People have mastered so much out there, and they all influence how we view and feel about life, and we can get caught up in the middle of things that are not about happiness. Man couldn't complete their masters, and opted in to anything that came their way, and at the end of the day, it does attract people or affect our lives, and if you are not sure of what you doing. You may not know what will happen to you, and the love you have in your heart, or for everything.

Human beings that are happy are always involved in sharing something genuine, and it not only exist between two people loving and making love. Yet it also exists within a flow of life that carries with it the power of true love, and is the theme of all that creates between lovers. It never takes a break, it is the heartbeat of creation, humanity, of every relationship and everyone that loves truly, of those who never stopped caring and believing in each other, for the rest of their lives.

So much about who we are is that we growing up moving forward, and for some time you might fail to recognize that change does occur, and neglect your responsibilities to be committed. Yet overtime we become experienced through our age, and when you come back with your need to love, you begin to realize that if I had never stopped loving. I would have been more than just happy, I could've lived a complete life. At the end we mustn't fail to live because of failing to understand why we're required to devote our lives to our partners early.

You will feel like you can relive your life, to find love when it was still young, and easy, but we only live once. To be fully content it needs one to deepen the degree of dedication towards understanding everything, and loving each other. The fact that you don't have to miss a moment to be happy, because of how impossible it can be to come back again, and join in on how things are.

I have never hesitated concerning how things have happened in this new age that we are now meant for one another, and if you don't understand how to truly give yourself to someone, you will learn along with learning how to respect creation.

Being alive is an opportunity to truly care for someone special, and if you ever miss that chance, you can become things which are not even worthy of who you are. True love herds our lives on a daily basis so that we don't get lost.

Believe in those who have seen and experienced things in this area of life, and save yourself the trouble of disappointment. It is all not worth it, you can struggle with the person that you are, that you choose to be, and decide what is it that matters when you reach the end.

You will get to understand that you can study everything there is in the world, yet there is no school of love, and discipline. It could either be common sense, or accept being told, you can live in any way and feel like it will make sense, but no it won't, nothing is a coincidence, you have to be loyal to this values, and virtues of creation.

Give more time to valuing a human being, and be precise in terms of resembling true love, so that you have one less thing to worry about. Accept to be guided through situations when life calls you back to focus, by saying, "remember that you are from the center of creation. If you want your path to be a decent one, then love is the channel that you need to follow".

I wish I knew why this part of our lives has such an effect on any individual, the giving of it all, and what makes it so impossible for a human to ever find someone that they truly care for. We all would have loved to know how important the other is, and loving one another truthfully, when the gift had to be shared at its true nature.

It doesn't matter who it is in the relationship who doesn't give in to it, but when you refuse to share it, at its true nature when you had to. A lot about love can pass you, and that which was available then, has now disappeared, and you will never be able to exchange it the way you were supposed to. The quality of life for human beings that walk in this world, is only enough for every man and woman, and all that they are, and for that special purpose that they have, so true love won't always be possible.

Sometimes you mustn't be passed by an opportunity to make love to each other if you had to, given that you can never know when that chance will be possible. Now you've allowed something truly amazing to pass you, which was only available for that moment and that day. You can try on another occasion only to realize that the unique opportunity can never be there again, it was only given once. The time it might take for you to meet on another occasion, so much could have happened, and the gift could have faded away.

At the end, we need to take every opportunity offered to be with one another and use it wisely, don't misuse the time you have to be with someone and share on a special moment of true love, or just to be making love. You might never have that experience available to you again, what can happen is, that tender situation can become a thing of the past. Of which you might never find easily, we all have something very important to give, a part of us that comes from deep within, and is the kind that can only be shared on a given occasion, through loving each other truly.

Give love and live it when it still matters, before you run out of options and be interrupted from finding your perfect lover. As it happens all the time when you can't meet someone to be with, that you do come across people, but the one you want to give yourself to is no longer there. Yet once in a lifetime you could have had that opportunity to have true love, and find your soul mate, something that is rare to achieve in this current existence.

Worse is that when you have died out of loving a human being, you can only come across people whom you can tolerate, even that is not easy. It becomes very difficult, to finally find someone that you understand, yet once in your life, that person was there, you could've been allowed a chance to be happy.

At times when situations were analyzed, I did understand something about a human being that we are all born with someone to love. However, along the way, you can have that particular individual taken away from you, that human has been very important in your life.

Yet when people have done so much to master their understanding until they pass the world, they can interrupt the flow of true love from combining you with that special part of you. That most imperative person can be anyone who passed through you, but not in the state which they were supposed to be when you were meant to find each other.

Still when you grow up you can overlook what you have lost before you can become active in loving a human being, and start another path somewhere. Our beginnings are usually very innocent, and you can happen to meet or find someone very important. So it's among this good tries that you can come across a special person or anyone worth living for, and if you don't ever lose that individual, you might be happy forever, because no matter how strong situation might be, you were born from love.

Love has been registered in our gins as something that is our birth right, you can only get caught when you haven't been honest and loyal in loving your partner. Other than that you can exercise your right to be loved, is when you have missed a chance to have done great things in resembling care for someone, that you can be found suffering from relationships and life's misfortunes. Nothing can take away that once in a lifetime opportunity to find true love, and happiness.

Chapter Nine

True love

We all belong to true love, it is our heart's most felt passion for our life's desires, if you cannot reach for that within the context of your understanding, Then you haven't find yourself, and your drive towards success, it is our point of transformation, We are mostly transformed by the love we have for who we are and what we do, it resembles our true value for everything in the world.

If you have not yet arrived at that point in your life, at that thrill which inspires you to move closer to your destiny, Then you haven't grasp the real power in you, that ability which puts you in control of your future. If you ever understand your real purpose, something that you want to live for your entire existence, then you have discovered your devotion to succeed.

A lot of people who are wandering, became lost because they had been denied an opportunity to love, and do others who have not yet find their true power for life. When you lack that inner drive, then you can't reach for your ambitions, your passion lived and understood. You feel and understand the world around you. All there is, you stand straight, tall, and content with understanding, as you strive to achieve your goals honestly, you will witness everything that you desire creating as you go forward through that love which you possess for it.

Learn to treasure your goals, don't ignore them even if is just for a day, or a single moment. Strive to discover the true meaning in whatever it is that you do, and to what living really means, and for some time you can forget that there is loving a person as our means to fullness.

While the real purpose is sharing our lives together as human beings, though a lot of people play with the chances they have to make each other happy. Without realizing that love is true, and those games that they entertain can become real-life obstacles, why? True love is a reality, and if it matters that much, then it comes from deep within our hearts and souls. So to be always content of yourself, don't be caught playing with things that you don't understand what they're worth, don't misuse an opportunity to please someone.

Happiness dwells within those regions of our inner-self, and nothing can ever take that away from us. If you haven't find yourself within the center of existence, on how to value a person, an opportunity to be joyful can pass you. However, if you strengthen yourself with complete devotion, you will be born again, and be able to stand strong with understanding in everything that you do.

This kind of knowledge about love serves a special purpose on how to clearly understand the meaning of everything in our daily basis. How important complete understanding of life, plays a role in achieving happiness in loving someone. The center is true love, and is always that which answers just about all the questions that we've ever had. The only thing that one needs is to know the truth, about ourselves towards each other, and when you've clearly find the value. Then we would be able to heal almost every part of our lives and never be stuck on matters of the heart again.

What if we have sinned in our lives or relationships? With all that we are to other human beings, but besides that we have been interrupted by jealousy and deception, and we can no longer love anything, or each other the way we use to. Can we start over again, and where do we begin? Given that we now know the truth about loving each other and ourselves.

When you couldn't find anyone to be with, you know that you opted for anything that came your way, and you understand that's not true about life and who we are. True love doesn't like creepy things or human beings that creep into other people when their desperate, or without a reason.

Always choose to be with someone who is enough for your entire existence, who becomes part of your vision, don't be caught in a relationship that is not what you want. Live with a well-defined objective in all areas of your life that could enable you to achieve all that you've ever desired. Sometimes you can pretend like you didn't know, while maybe you knew, you just didn't understand the effect thereof, but that doesn't mean you won't account for those mistakes.

For some time living without a partner might not be painful, yet as you keep unfolding into the central core of humanity. You then begin to feel the pain, it could be constant, or maybe slow because of how things are. You looking at the center where life is forever flowing, where love takes no break, and you wonder how can one ever becomes part of something so glorious through own understanding. Is when you find yourself left-back or behind schedule of your progress, and you have no one to lean on, and you must rely on your knowledge to breakthrough reality again.

You can't say is what you want to understand or what one is doing, at times our hearts cannot easily heal from a setback, or a heartbreak, and whatever we follow around our lives is affected by that. You feel so caged from failing to understand how to truly give yourself to someone, you stand and watch everything moves on, dwelling in that moment of sadness. Knowing very well your past failures are not the solution, and you can never rest on anything. You have to get up, give it all the courage that you have, and if love has different angles, then find a new path that leads to it as your ultimate destiny.

All the people who knows that you deserve better, or exercise your beliefs and struggling with reaching the center, do not stop now while you know what you have is not the answer. Even though you experience hardships, because the world hasn't offered you anything, to a better future or to live through, it doesn't matter. Knowing very well that whatever your efforts have paid you is not enough. However, keep on striving to find true love worthy of you.

Life is something that requires attention, time, dedication, commitment, and understanding, and then with love you come out of the dead through that certainty which describes exactly what you are, and the kindness of your heart, to be a human being so full of tender.

I can try to explain what I've got to understand after a defined period of time, so much can be said about love, you can either have that kind of affection for yourself first, or something will fail. You can die everywhere from everything, except in that feeling you have for oneself, it is that strong, it can keep a human being alive, no matter how dead you feel. True love, when you have it, becomes elementary to life, regardless of how bad situations can be. It has that pillar of strength that can provide you with a way to rediscover your purpose again.

Without love where is true so much has been taken away from you. Yet from deep within, you can discover a new path that lies in the depth of your soul that calls for you to focus on creating a lot of good with your heart. Even if you don't know where to start, you can always begin right here inside yourself, with what you want to achieve. These were among the paths which I had discovered, which are the most incredible, and perfectly amazing ways which can bring a human being back to reality. To respect yourself, life, and to be committed to what you want to see.

I was a man with a purpose, I had chosen to be one, with no need to substitute that for any reason, I had no regrets for anything that I was, and which I had been doing. I lived to see my own creativity form into reality, yet you find yourself disappointed at times, and from that anger could have try to live in me, or just to build a home inside.

Somehow I didn't care about so much, as long as I was in the path which was necessary to reach for my goals. You can try to find, or make peace with all that is happening around, then I got to understand that maybe is the outcome of what you doing that matters at the end of the day.

To be content of yourself again there is so much that one needs to really think of, where do we find ourselves, when we have died from the challenges of this gigantic world? I know that what I had didn't mean much, yet all that I am kept longing to understand everything that can lead someone back to reality through that path of your desires.

The beauty of your knowledge in understanding life, commitment, love, and romance, these are the four elements of happiness, when there is nothing left in a human being. Then the question comes, how do you work around this concepts to find who you are once more, where do you begin?

Things can emerge from every direction, and you must be alert, whichever comes first might need you to hold on tight. Though knowledge about life is hard to find and can be isolated in its approach, and it can stand before every desire you have. However, if you can achieve that, you hold the key to unlock everything that is love, romance, and commitment.

Then at the end of the day, you realize how important our goals are when you need to find yourself, regardless of how so much can keep pulling you back from getting that fulfillment. The most crucial part is to recognize what can help you triumph through every difficulty. So that when an opportunity arises you can grow with everything, given that you know how it feels to live without direction to a better future.

You could have find yourself stuck, and eager to understand exactly what it is that you doing, and how to do it right. That is without having to mention what could have gone wrong, yet everything begins with love, situations always breaks there, and before you know you can't repair the damage. If is not about how you neglected someone, then is how you have been resented by the one you trusted the most, or what you have not done right along the way.

When you have failed to be content of yourself through relationships, it could be because that part is dependent on the other, however, life is our own responsibility. You must learn to handle that side of yourself on your own, that doesn't depend on another person, it depends on you, to make good out of situations. We have very limited opportunities to find a good partner, you could've failed in love, and however, the way back to it again could be through mastering your own understanding.

It begins with you, as a way of picking up the pieces back to reality, through your own understanding and love for oneself you are building a solid foundation for your future. It means a lot to understand who you are, yet it might not mean that you will have the whole world, and it doesn't guarantee complete happiness. So don't lose focus on true love, chasing after power and trying to have control over everything, just be happy you becoming a human being again, a person so full of life, and valid to be in a worthy relationship.

Regardless of the time we live in, always figure out different ways to reach your goals, and arrive at the center of creation. Given that everything out there has a force, and so much could try to block the way to your destiny.

Yes it won't happen overnight, it could be that is your ideas, and they mean a lot to the person that you are, and it might become the only way available for you to matter. You could have suffered a great loss of love, and died out of all that the world is offering, and becoming meaningless from this ordinary life which everyone belongs to. Now your own path is here to make you a human being again, and with true love in your heart, you can transform everything into success.

I had chosen a path for myself, which I could say that it didn't matter what situation had produced at some point, as long as it was a route to my own destiny, and moving forward towards love. It was another way to say that I couldn't live my life to destruction, if it can get me to where I'm headed then is fine, it is a road to success. I had spent almost three years without anyone to give myself to, and I had felt myself becoming very lonely in my journey.

Though you feel this unnecessary hesitation, however, I had now passed the first doorway to my deepest self, I can say that I had pass somewhere, that even if I could try to live in denial of what I understand, I couldn't go back. I had to work at things from that angle to the end, ahead the future promised to be very bright.

With or without anyone to commit myself to, after a very long time, something in me had already begun to develop, it was love for creativity and all that exists, and I did take it serious. As it had a significant purpose to serve, it had brought happiness back to my life, and that's how everything is supposed to be. You know when you get to that part where your desires begin to make sense, when you had been striving a long time for something that you believe in. Now things begins to be fulfilling as you understand what you doing completely, when certainly so much becomes simple.

No matter what the world or everybody says, I didn't want to waste any time, thinking that there could have been better ways to live my life or do things. Though I had been knocked out by love before, I couldn't spend the rest of my existence wondering about loving someone. I had discovered a path that was very inspirational and a purpose to dedicate all my attention to. I had find true love on my own, for our lives, and everything that comes with it, an objective to serve that was always fulfilling.

To live with a purpose led by love wasn't easy, along the way, so much becomes difficult to pass through, and you will feel like pausing and changing who you are. In my head, and deep in my heart, I knew how to lead myself to a good direction, and I had done everything in my power to remain focus, and with confidence it was a great life. Which I valued with everything that I had, and it was important to me as it was something that I had invented on my own, and if it was to become reality, then someone would follow, and another would cling on to me for that.

Life had now become the ultimate love in my heart, alone though it couldn't do much, it had done enough for me to envy the way back to reality. For some time I wasn't really involved with things, I had neglected myself, yet through the eagerness to be creative, I had discovered a new way and a worthwhile purpose to live for. From that I became a human being again, for a certain period I kept on living while loving who I am only. Deep inside I was confident knowing that what I now hold explains all the parts of creation, and everything that I value as well.

I had now find value in myself, it was in those early years where you not sure of what you doing. You are only holding on to love and fewer things out of this creative atmosphere, and you can say that you still learning, and is good to learn when it is shaping your future for the better.

It is very meaningful when it is giving you a chance to find a better way on how to begin all that your life comprises of. Given the fact that it is a tough journey out there, as so much could need you to be patient for a very long time before you can see everything that you doing. A lot could come in the most uncertain period, and when a human being doesn't fully understand what they're doing, you just become lost. I think whether experimental or not, the answer will always be one, it's meant to be part of learning because having to discover your path can never be that easy.

It was in those years where there had been something that I had been doing as well, which at the beginning meant nothing. Yet from that, a new world was invented, and it became my point of transformation, it was part of what wouldn't truly be expected to ever lead to a greater path which could change someone's life. However, knowledge transformed everything into a magnificent beautiful creation, a new way of creating things became a reality. A route that approaches creativity through healing, and all that which I had been involved in, began to be recognized from that.

Love is truly a miracle, or rather something very amazing, not a thing that anyone would easily grasp, it can change your entire understanding. When things begin to make sense, is the only thing that you will find being creation out there, and then you realize that when on that premature stage, everything that you understood was not real.

Is true, if you can learn to sort out all the misunderstanding that you facing, you will see the outcome being true love, and that will change what you doing for the better. It has the power to take something from nothing, and turn it into a valuable entity. Through commitment and sacrifice for that desired thing, your ambitions becomes clearer. Right there when you think you can't be useful any more, apply the law of kindness and come back to being a person that matters.

So much will want to weigh you down as everything has a servant, and all these impossible ways of dealing with things, serves the purpose of destruction. You can't work to destroy the person that you are, when you are in your right state of mind, is true, our entire efforts have a specific objective, whether conscious or not. So imagine living life without love, and what you doing to yourself, you're destroying everything that you value.

I know for sure with love and life things are not easy to understand, and nothing makes sense, so it could be said that it is the longest journey throughout our entire existence. Together they disappear into the depths of our soul, and so much could want to hold you back along the way, failure to manage everything too early can influence the rest of your path. I was truly into valuing what I am or what I do, and when something wasn't right, I knew how to stay away from it.

To be caught up or stuck in this world of love, you see things become what you didn't expect, there's so much that influences this part of reality. I was not loved by anything at some point, and I remained like that longer than I could bear, I wished every day to have seen something good or different, and still there was none.

I had things that had built dependency among who I am, and I couldn't live it behind, I had to carry it through with me. At the end I had to allow transformation to occur, through participation and commitment in everything that I did. Then later when everything had become a reality, I was able to understand that a lot defies the reality that we know about things.

When I had seen the world to the end, then there was no need for me to be strong for any purpose. Yet love, the only reason why you must never give up on anything, pushes you to strive for success through the path you have chosen, as a lot dies as we proceed ahead. You understand very well that you cannot give up on it, though at times it might feel as if is too hard to achieve, as things becomes heavy to live with.

You can live this life thinking that there's any better solution anywhere in the world, but there's none, love is the answer, our point of surrender, for those who undertake, the purpose of it, are destined to find happiness at the end.

As you keep on working and fixing things, do it with love, knowing that this is the best life, and at the end, you can never guess what the universe can provide to you. You will achieve everlasting joy, as it is not only important to the cause in which you have taken, for yourself to find a clear path, or someone to commit to. However, it matters to the whole of humanity, you are helping in restructuring hope in the world.

Although it is something that I didn't know the importance of when I was young, now I am aware of the value thereof. I am at the edge of creation, and creativity the way it must be done, and doing it in such a way that everybody will come to admire and understand you perfectly.

After I reached a certain stage I had begun to understand the purpose of devoting myself to what I was doing, it had led me out of difficult situations. To be fully content of what was required of me, had pulled me out of this dark hole where I had been stuck forever, through lacking knowledge. When your mind becomes imprisoned as you lack answers to what living really means.

I was completely in the dark, the depth of the concept life, had left me heartbroken, and my soul darkened at a very early age. At first I didn't realize the significance of what it really meant, yet, as I was growing and began to believe more, a lot changed. From that angle of caring about myself and so much that I was doing, I could see the world clearly, then I began to understand everything well. To just be devoted to what I was, had come as a sort of encouragement. Something that motivates me to discover who I am on a deeper level, and all that matters easily, the world responded better from that facet of reality.

I could have given up on everything that matters, only that life is not worth giving up on, one might look at love as a way to be with someone. Yet in essence, when you begin to devote yourself to what you want with everything that you have on a daily basis. You get to realize that there's more that you offering through that kindness of the heart than what a person can make of. You plant a seed of happiness inside, and not just for a single day, if nourished, forever, because to all that we work hard for, true love is free.

A very courageous path towards creation, one you can use to tackle situations, and to never tire on what you have begun. A way in which you can rejuvenate yourself with, it begins as a means to find sense in all that you doing. The best motivational discipline that reduces the frustrations of our lives into a clear route, and from that I had founded myself something I can dedicate my whole attention, to completely fall in with the whole of creation. A very constructive way in which I can grow stronger into focusing on everything that I am and what I do.

Through understanding how to hold love tenderly in my heart, I had come back from the world of being hopeless, and it had brought joy back into my life. A setback from a committed relationship can bring discouragement that you might fail to understand, a lot call it depression, when your mind stops thinking ahead.

You become blindfolded by situations, in terms of focusing in the future, and you start dwelling in your old age. Yet even in this past of yours, you are only focused on the negative things which you have done, which could have led to the situation that you're in, and the worse part you continuously fail to pass that period.

There had been greatest moment, where I would remember everything good about life, yet my mind would constantly crawl back to that past incident again. I had lost love at a very early age, but even when I had acquired a lot of lessons, motivation, and understanding about relationships, I still went back to that place where my heart had collapsed.

I kept dwelling in that heartbreak, and not even a new relationship could help me to work my way out of that broken situation. It had become an emotional struggle, or a spiritual battle that I had to face daily, and then I realized that nothing passes to reality until it has passed through your entire being.

One of the most important things I had to understand is that whatever you have lost can never be found once more. You have to build something from the scratch, a new human being birthed by love, who will be alive, and made to understand the values of commitment. Given that to go through such a loss of true love is death in spirit, and whatever has died cannot be offered a chance to live again, that which is dead must be put to rest.

That kind of loss carries its dignity in spirit into reality, it always reflects that something important has left your whole being, and only true love has the power to give birth to whatever you have lost before. Is that love for everything, yourself, life, and someone special, is to treasure all that matters in this beauty of the world that you have discovered in you.

You take it with you, put it in your heart and cherish it with your entire existence, until you reach at that point of transformation. Where you transform through the devotion you carry inside, and that commitment pushes you back to reality as a new creation, a human being who lives with true value for understanding.

Time has pressure on us to come back to reality, though we all eat what has died, and we could have enjoyed everything that death has fed us. You cannot remain dead forever, you have to find your toehold, as some could lead us back to life, because they are not meant to kill, still, the world won't make it easy for you to be a human being in love again.

There is a huge negative force that can be produced by a lack of pulse. When you were out of the circulation of love, you lived against the flow as you are without a loving relationship. Now when you want to come back to being a person that matters to someone, it might be difficult. Given that whatever has killed true love in your heart, won't make it easy for you to be involved with another again.

As the world circulates and moving on with human beings loving and making love, everyone within an active relationship must move at the same level of passion for life. So imagine if you had been sharing that kind of feeling with someone, and without being prepared for anything, you disappear out of that splendor?

Then you're instantly cut-off from everything that exists, while people continue to share themselves with one another, with dedication to pleasing each other. While you remain behind, and time follows to get the best out of you, hoping for salvation or anyone to save you, and there won't be any, or it might not happen overnight. It takes a long period to recover from that kind of setback, and so much can turn against you before you find the right person again.

Love can take a timeless journey into manhood or womanhood, and you remain behind with no one, and to be specific on the matter, can you imagine being knocked out from relationships at a certain age? And now you don't even know how to come back to be with someone, through lack of motivation and attention on the issue from anyone, because it isn't easy to confront human beings about this kind of issues.

When you die out of true love and everything that comes with it, so much can come to pass, and relationships can provide a lot for someone to mature, and if all that has passed, you might be permanently left back. As the world can never stop loving and living, and a great deal could happen while you continue with being human elsewhere, and you just can't join in the flow of love when you want to. Creation can run down on you like a wheel of life, and you might never experience being with another so easy.

The bad part about relationships is that once your age passes, you can never catch up on the same thing, you have to wait for a different group. Which might be young or old, to enter with you into their cycle of love, as creation respects what you have lost. You can't be left broken forever, though you could be judged for the person that you have become, and the world can choose to continue even on the next given opportunity to ruin your chances of happiness. Things can turn to be hard to find a good partner especially one who is not the same generation with you.

It becomes rather unusual when two people not in the same age group must fall in love with one another, as the other is forced to find a good relationship, of which you can hardly get in the same generation level, or where you use to be. At times you can wonder how someone can come back to falling with the right person again, how do you start all over again, when true love has been circulating for a very long time? Could it be that you need to master everything that you doing so that you are not easily challenged. Being able to reflect a reason for arriving late, other than to be knocked out of life from not valuing things.

It is very crucial to understand the importance of time in determining a human being's life back to the world. As you cannot always be young, and how you dearly stand alone in finding a way to be a human in love again. We can say that a person has been born traveling at the same pace with his age, no matter what you have been busy with, you can never be doing it alone. So there is no harm in birth, it all belongs within the same flow in which we have been born free from true love. However, if it's about the failure in relationships and loving someone, then everyone has passed, they have grown up, left you behind, you are now on your own.

If you can master life, and the subject of loving a human being, success, and what you can produce, as part of your understanding, it can mean everything, it can be a new beginning. So what if you haven't mastered everything and you have died out of the deepest love humanity can ever understand? And you want your way back into romance, and you can never be easily accepted, unless you have been given the best of all the love that man and woman can ever have. Maybe you might need to surrender, be subject to circumstances of this world, as things can never be impossible to handle, we all go through challenges that are enough for who we are.

Once your age group has passed, you can never catch up on the same thing, rather be that you've learned to accept whatever comes your way. It would be so much better if maybe you have been studying how to be disciplined, in doing what you find necessary, as love can just give you anything there is available. So at the end of the day when you've mastered life, I guess that you can find answers to the question where relationships had been posing threats, and surprise you with something worthy.

Though at times it depends on how you mastered your understanding, if you have studied within an institution and becoming a master. That could be able to save your soul given that you have a lot of options, unlike with some masters where you study on your own. Things can turn to be very difficult as you have to stand apart from the rest of the people and everyone who could want to oppose you.

The end must clearly define or distinguishes your knowledge from everything and everyone who exists out there. Especially when you haven't obtain that kind of understanding from an institution, you must be focused on creating a subject that represents your own point of view. Otherwise you can really see your world begins to fall apart on whatever it is that you try to achieve, or in anything that you try to be part of you feel very challenged.

Is when you are not the ultimate solution to what you require, and there's a need for other people's input, in order to figure a way out of your problems. An independently complete masters must be able to stop the time and how things had been creating in the world to enable you to find a place where you belong. You know that part where everything stops and you are able to join in the flow of creation and you begin to move forward with everyone, and you are generously welcome.

That's your new community or the level where you can begin your life now, unlike having to force your ideas on human beings. The world can be pushed to destruct, is when you have become unfamiliar with current situations, you can turn to be too much of a destruction in people's lives.

I mean the truth about love did exist before, yet you couldn't find yourself within that context, and you could have found your soul mate, or maybe you could have become the most irrelevant person to the time in which we live in. Can you imagine trying to fit into a certain lifestyle while you still have so many questions and to the most obvious issues?

Now that you have gain knowledge of what the world has come to, and you can see everything clearly. When you have mastered everything accordingly, and how things are, and you were able to close the gap that can exist when you are left behind, and being relevant to the time in which we currently live our lives, life and love became easy.

Chapter Ten

Spark of Love

Love is rather amazing, something you cannot fully grasp or fulfill in one encounter, even if you can try, there's just a lot that needs to be done, and one day is not enough. The things you need to accomplish when loving each other are so much, that you require a second chance to do everything right. Every day is another turn that you get to achieve all that which must be done and appropriately.

You deserve a new opportunity every day of your life to perform at your best level, to resemble a lot that you needed the other to see, that you might had forgotten. That you thought of as you wanted to get to a certain point that would please your lover, where your love can produce happiness for both of you, and be able to reach for true love.

Even when approaching someone for the first time, you might fail to put all that you wanted clearly into perspective. Yet you might find a way on how to win the situation, by creating a mutual understanding, or maybe have a way to reach an agreement with each other. Every day of our lives is a new opportunity to try and make each other happy, as you can never fulfill everything at once. You continue with giving more as you go by, and perhaps you can find some closure with ever doing things the way they need to be done, you must be given enough chance to work through each other's hearts.

You can worry yourself about what you never did right, at times we are not given enough opportunity to do what we want, or to prove our love. A day is only enough for so much that you can be able to demonstrate or say about yourselves. A good loving relationship is a commitment to give in to each other every day and minute of our lives. You continuously require one another so that you can satisfy the hunger for something that you both feel the need to share.

You wouldn't want to lose the only treasure you ever valued with your whole heart because you failing to please the other. So if in other instances it calls for a true communion to be painful, and discipline, let it be, both serves a purpose of true love. It is unbearable to be without someone who looks into your every need, yet exercising care can restore happiness in our daily being.

Fulfill the objectives of a commitment the way it must be done, prepare yourself for one another every day, bring the enthusiasm of life to each other. Look at a new day as a chance to please your lover more than you did yesterday, let love grow stronger on a daily basis because you nurture it with true devotion and dedication.

After all, other than relationships we exist for so much, and it is only complete when you live your lives fully. There is stress that can be produced by the jobs that we do, and you can't neglect to work as it is the only thing we're meant for outside communions. So if it has anything to do with achieving happiness and satisfaction, then people must be free to do whatever they like.

Only apply discipline, and do it for the right reasons, we are not meant for everything, you can't do as much as you want out there and still win in your relationship. With some you will lose, and when you come back with that into your love life, you weaken all that you value, in a commitment you don't have to put the other through that.

You are required to bring confidence, true love, and happiness into each other's lives, if you're eager to win your partner's heart, you need to consider one another very well. You must be able to hold yourself back when dealing with issues inside and outside your communion, you are not the only one in the cycle, your lover can get hurt.

Then comes the different opinions that we have, some can be fixed, while others cannot be settled at all, it becomes the end of everything that we have been doing. At some point you feel that you need to try and be a better person, yet situations could be worse than you can handle, and anger keeps boiling inside. Still, somehow you have to be disciplined for your family needs you, and you can't go back to being a single person. What happens when you no longer understand each other, does it mean it's over, where do we find the courage to be happy again, and continue with love the way it was?

Things can continue worsening until you realize that there is nothing remaining for you in this relationship, and growth can be pulling you back to realize that your decision can cost you a lot. That you must choose your way carefully, knowing it is the best possible solution, that's what ruins the spark of love, everything that can happen in our lives, just to mess up the happiness we have. You can't predict the future or know all that there is about life, yet you need to be prepared enough for so much that there is to keep in mind about each other.

Once again everything that you have in your house has been ruined by what you've brought from outside your household, and you can never know the results of all that you doing, that can change things in your lives. Relationships are very fragile and they can collapse from anything that we do, and you end up stuck, asking yourself how am I supposed to find the spark of love again? Something that can clear the confusion that you both feeling within you, and how can we mend our broken hearts or make things right?

True love is not for the weak hearted, so many times you will want to quit and be a new person, or else you have to learn to confront situations and make things right. Although you cannot pretend like you are someone who doesn't understand what you doing, always remember that you can know too much, only to lose the war on love.

With relationships you can be disappointed at times, and having to live with such disappointments, can make one feel like their life has been betrayed and undermined. Then there is this issue not like anything we have ever seen, it keeps on happening to us, most especially in this new age that we exists in because things have changed eventually.

We became too exposed when it comes to love, and you could see that it will need more than just discipline to be able to find true love, and how can it be possible with everything against our lives? You may understand or be sure of what to do, but that's what makes situations worse, the more you know, the bigger the problem that you facing. There was so much that had begun interfering within our relationships, especially when you seek someone who can settle down with you.

It doesn't matter that you are a man or a woman, honestly you can come across a certain situations that you can refuse to be honest to yourself about. Not every relationship is based on true love, and you too can get caught up in that kind of a dilemma, that the other wants you just for fun, and there could be a lot to lose. Deep down inside you know that you have love, and you want someone who can give you all that you deserve.

That can become heavy on you, when you can't deal with emotions very well, as you need to make a sound decision. It hurts when a person refuses to commit, and changes the nature of things and honesty between one another. Though there could be different reasons why one might not be willing to give in to what you are, and why they don't want to be committed at that time.

It could be about anything that you don't have or maybe something you don't understand, makes you feel bad about yourself too. You could be a nice person, is just that love isn't blind, and it questions a lot about who you are, and you cannot live to your full potential in terms of being in a relationship. It is clear to see that this kind of engagement with one another is settling for less, only that it is what is available at the moment, and there's no true love, as the other cannot see through your heart, and yes you want commitment, but not now.

Then the question comes, are you missing something that you cannot be normal without, or is there anything important that you were supposed to do, which you not doing? It could be that you are not where you need to be right now, so much comes as an achievement and you must earn it, so it is with relationships as well. I wanted to understand the difference between love and what you feel when you are not completely in it with your whole heart, and what pushes someone to commit to the other, is it money, status, beauty, or maybe true love?

We live in difficult times where true love is not enough, so much has become attached to it, and for someone seeking for commitment is never too late to do what you want, or whatever it is that can increase your confidence. You can get to where you attract love by understanding clearly what you are, don't accept anything less than what you really deserve. All that which you will come across along the way amounts to nothing, compared to what you need.

The world has changed so much, even if you are not part of it now, but after some time that person whom you think exist in you, disappears, and you can't do it anymore. Sometimes love comes from being satisfied with everything that there is in our lives, that's where we get the confidence to resemble the quality of life required to find true love.

No matter how strong you might feel the need to keep dating one another for fun out there, comes a situation where you must surrender everything that you doing. Somewhere along the way you have to settle down, yet you know that you will engage for a marriage, but there could be times where you refuse to be engaged because you still enjoy playing as man and woman. Then when you reach the end you want someone who is fully dedicated to love.

It might happen that you don't easily come across such a person, given that you were once not prepared for those kind of responsibilities. There is only one opportunity to commit and to have physically or spiritually make yourself ready for everything in a relationship. At times is not about the physical contact or presence only, we all have that undying need for love, is like, within a loving commitment, you can be able to rest your whole life and feel calm or home free.

You have to search for a solution to love, which is true to your heart, and not about everyone, one only meant for you to be happy. Given that it is not funny when you constantly seek for someone whom you don't know where they will come from. You wanted to find great things in the world, and you can't have them all, can you? A human being is a different story altogether.

You will come back later only to realize that you have acquired a lot, only that you couldn't acquire true love. You keep going on with life and to every direction that you must be heading, looking for someone that you can rely on. Even though it's rare to find people or anyone that you can trust into a relationship with you, a person who can give all that they are, you keep hoping for a good outcome if you know you've done things right along the way.

Loneliness can get the better of you, the thing is, you can set your mind on something that represents everything that you truly desire, and you never find your way back to the world you use to know. You keep trying yet the path is closed, there's just no going back to your childhood, you heading straight to the end of your life.

You enter new chapters of your life, knowing that what you doing will not get any better soon, regretting the path you have begun. If you had just searched for someone to love, you would have achieved happiness right at the beginning, and the most painful thing is when you know what you want to achieve even in a relationship. So if you truly seek a good partner, you keep going on until you become a product of true love, and see all that you are become formed by loving a human being.

You have faith that what you doing will yield good results at some point, and the outcome of it is something that you lived for, the rest of your life. By now you can't tell the difference between your personal goals and that of your relationships, they all depend on the same thing, of you reaching success. Which one matters the most?

Both wouldn't come easy, yet if you preserve everything, you conclude what you doing very well, and you would live to be happy, rather than to go on with regrets. Better if you can see that there is light at the end of the tunnel, than being stuck in complete darkness, of which can make you feel miserable and pointless to keep on living.

In the path you have chosen you know what you doing, and you confident in yourself because you believe in the outcome of everything thereof. You cannot escape your ideas, and you can't delegate, it's your responsibility to the end. You acknowledge that you could have so much that you wanted, but you have that standing in your way for good and for worse.

So a solution can only be invented through your understanding, and that is what you have faith in, and you can meet someone to be with before you get there. Only to find that they are not interested in your ideas or visions, they want to see something concrete, as everyone wants to fall in love with a finished product.

Then you realize that the end is more important to what you want, than what you can say about yourself. Along the way there is nothing that you understand permanently, and for everyone that comes into your life. Yet to complete everything is for you and everyone to see exactly, how true love has formed through your understanding.

There is so much that passing this youth can represent, what have you given up, that at times you felt like you can go back and start afresh? I gave up my whole youth as I wasn't content of what it is that I was doing, and chose a way to a better future. Besides being young at that time I started something that changed my entire world, although it came with responsibilities, but it was worth everything that I risked, given that it was meant to last forever.

I had to watch so much come to pass because it wasn't who I am and what I needed to achieve, is just that when you want your ideas to come alive. Then you need to have faith in them more than any human being, no matter how much situations can try to question your beliefs. You keep believing in your invention about life, as you are the only one who has the power to carry your way of understanding to reality.

Even when it comes to our lives is like that, the world is a battle when you not inside your home, and is all that you will ever go through. So the most important thing for you to know is that, everything outside your household is for life, and that's how a day goes. It starts and you head out there to face reality, forget about the person that you love the most, and be part of creation as it moves on, and for some time you have to put it behind you. Whether you've found true love or not you have to let it be and focus on being a productive individual.

Yes you are loved, only that you mustn't fail to stand your own ground and do exactly what is required of you. Yet you look at the world in a rush, as you could be in a hurry to go back to your comfort zone, but outside you need to be an independent individual, and not to hate whatever it is that you doing. A lot of people that have found true love cannot remain straight and strong, however, if you can apply all that you've learned, you could be very effective.

You must learn to be strong and do your part, but besides that, so many people uses true love for their partners, as their only armor when facing situations, and they become very weary, as early as possible, your body become exhausted very fast. It longs to reunite with the love that it has on the inside, whereas on the other hand, there's knowing what you doing. If you put that where it must be as your weapon towards confronting with the world, you produce excellent results.

So if you have found true love for the world and everything that you know how to be, that can never disappoint or be taken away from you. If you're truly certain of everything that you doing, it is all the love that you require to start something magnificent. You never get tired from doing what you passionate about, as you engaging in it with your whole heart, and that is what you need to reach for success in both family and life. You have cycled your entire activities with genuine understanding, and that gives you the energy to deal with whatever it is that has been delegated to you.

To complete this is to find someone who can help you to parent everything, giving you the ultimate love for what you know and believe in, as well as everything that you deserve, and making you happy ever after. The secret comes from loving yourself first, as well as your family, what can satisfy someone is when you have done whatever you need according to the passion you have for all that exists. To what extent did what you started mean, and if what you doing means everything to you, what did you go through to test your belief?

You have taken your own path given that out there, there's something that you permanently despise with your whole heart. Before you could even develop your special purpose, you still knew that you had to do what you must to avoid this way. Knowing very well it was not how your life was intended to be at the beginning.

Is how I had experienced the world as an individual, don't lose hope on the belief that you have, even when it feels as if is an impossible situation, you have to remain faithful. Though things might be difficult sometimes, yet it is something you can keep learning more about as you move forward. You could be without proper understanding, but what it means is that you don't want what is been offered, and so much gets exciting when you begin to understand everything better and becoming a little intelligent on the subject that you have created.

As you begin to better understand whatever it is that you doing, you keep moving closer to the center where you become easy to love. Someone who gets to live with everyone very well and simpler than before you could know yourself more, as you now resemble a lot of intelligence. At times even in relationships you can bring that sense of understanding and security that your partner feels safe around you.

Although there was no commitment along the way, now you are the driver, and you know where you headed, you are heading somewhere so wonderful, that life cannot deny you anything on the path you have chosen. All you have to do is to learn to appreciate and treasure every opportunity you get to be sharing love with a special being and grow with it.

You look tired and strained from trying to understand how to fit your way into life, and all you need is someone whom you can truly commit to, and when you get that, give something really meaningful. Have so much to offer, that a person can never be bored of you, show each other true love, you have fought your battles to find one another and you have won, and now it's time to win it within your hearts.

That is how the world will make sense with everything that you've been doing, don't just give a little of who you are, but more than required, and not to be bored of love. As it is where the beauty lies, so enjoy it, even if not committed yet, only that you can seize the moment and be satisfied with loving the other.

Chapter Eleven

Love Drops

So many people fear loving each other as they think that somehow the other partner is going to disappoint them, and they will be left broken hearted. Which in real life is true since you can never know what a person is thinking or capable of doing on the other side.

So when you begin to love, though you want to carry it all with you for the rest of your life, you can hold back as you could be afraid of disappointments. Remember that you are not loving for you to be disappointed, you are carrying yourselves through to the end of your lives, not hoping for any setbacks along the way, is true love for each other until death.

To get to a point where you understand how to surrender yourselves, you must be able to accommodate love, your heart must be free to commit. So if you somehow still have this huge feeling of fear, of being afraid of betrayal, you not there yet. A worthwhile relationship must be able to let you rest easily, you must give yourself to someone who values your presence in their lives, who doesn't take advantage of your absence.

The true foundation of happiness is being with someone who cares about you, who understands what you giving, your lover must be easy to love. The person who deserves your heart doesn't need to be monitored in order to do the right thing, they know the value of a partner in a relationship is to be trustworthy.

All that which we give to one another must be secured, you just can't let go of everything that you value like that, and to love must be insured, by an insurance that can save you from heartbreaks. The thing is when you've been hurt before, or maybe you had been cheated by your partner, your heart becomes so fragile. It always fears that it could get hurt, and you might fail to stand the pain again, and that makes it so hard to ever commit.

What really causes a heartbreak? Is when someone that you truly love and trusts with all that you are, cheats on you deliberately. Knowing very well that you dwell in their heart and you care about them so much, they go out with another person, or even commit a sexual offense with the other being aware of how you feel about them. Is when you've cared about a human being a lot that you value their presence with everything that you are, and then something goes wrong with the intention to harm. That is what pushes a human to break down, and fail to ever trust in a relationship again.

So when it comes to committing to a different person, you never make a mistake, being afraid that you could go through the same situation of heartbreaks and you might hurt yourself badly. Deep within your sub consciousness you always remember that a human being can commit a sexual offense. So when you're involved with someone, before they cheat, or engages with another, your heart always rejects that individual.

So that if they fornicate, it happened outside the cycle of your commitment, to avoid having to go through the pain of being broken-hearted. That's how you can save yourself from breaking once more, and from there you begin to strengthen your inner-self to trust even more. Regardless of whether it is in a communion or not, as it has been forever evident that the function of who we are is to continuously care. So if you can never be broken again, you continue to harness the everlasting joy that you have planted inside, and it is meant to keep growing stronger every day.

It will only exist in your mind that someone can intentionally try to hurt, or cheat on you, yet it can never depress you. In your head, you must be able to handle all the pressure of knowing that a person can reject you, without having to tell you first. It always works like magic, you can't be rejected forever, and when your heart learns to dive out of a situation like that, love doesn't become a stroke of bad luck.

It only becomes a curse when someone committed a sexual offense within the cycle of your relationship. That can turn out to be the most hurting situation you've ever had to face, and you can live with it for the rest of your life. Is like breaking a mirror, it can never be fixed again, no heart can break and be repaired that easy, the reflection of it, also changes the shape of your reality.

So as a results, a lot of people are very frightened to commit themselves to their partners, yet in essence man and woman mustn't be scared to love. Knowing that when someone drops you, another will catch you, if it's deep then true love will be there, and to sustain you over that period. Is truly something that you can rely on, even if you've been hurt before, it could be during a period where you find that you hurting and fail to recognize anyone ready to commit to you. Maybe there could be a way for one to see, when life situations refuses to outsmart human beings and make them feel like they don't belong or deserve to be loved.

Yet we find ourselves blindfolded by those who have mastered this way of living, since they believe in deceiving human beings and breaking their hearts. However, man and woman must be prepared to love, they mustn't be left to break, and they must be brought closer to each other. Even in times when they're still confused, so that you not taken down that path of believing that something is too wrong and cannot be fixed.

You can be healed by other human beings with greater understanding, who have joined in the act of doing good, instead of deceiving people and exploiting their feelings even when is not necessary. Love has a tendency of giving everything that it has to those who need it most, for life would like for you to know, or see that you are not lost on any occasion. That true love will always be there to protect you from harm, and you mustn't be held back by your past experiences, which have hurt you and left you torn apart.

I believe so many that grew up outside Christianity only to find themselves in this way of life, have had the same experience of not believing too much in their partners at first, when they had just began loving each other. It was after the experience that we usually go through of losing what we had, that breeds all this immoral behaviour in relationships, that we began taking love and commitment very seriously and started to resemble true love for one another.

Here where we are today, is the world in between that has the power to sustain a human being who needs love, for you mustn't be easily misled by situations. That calls you into a misbehaving way of life, as you no longer inside Christianity, it is not the end for you to find happiness, you worthy of greater things. You have a lot of potential, and you're still a valid person, the universe has so much to offer and that platform is open for whatever you desire.

Situations cannot hurt you forever, if you can just discover a purpose to live for, something that can arouse the passion for everything. You will understand that there is more than one kind of love, there's true love in this world, and you can find it for whatever determination you have.

In this new way that we've discovered, where we are mostly formed by our past experiences and failures from our true desires, and what we wanted to live for. Is where you need to stop and think about what you truly need, and not to be in a hurry, do not run and give in to what you don't really want, it is a breaking period, where you are required to rest.

Here we can make a living, we can find joy in all that we doing, and you can never believe that everyone is scared of disappointments. No one wants to put their life at risk, however, at this stage, you can be able to rehabilitate yourself from your setbacks and be on the healing process, for you cannot be left broken for eternity.

This is where so much has been made not to worsen, given that a lot of people love taking advantage of the situations that human beings find themselves in, and exploiting them not to ever find happiness in whatever they seek to be. Once you lose someone, your put at the center of creation, so to have your patience tested on every level, and whether you have the mental ability to cope with difficulties, and failure to apply any of the strength of the virtues of love. You just give up on everything and disappear into a world where you have failed to reach success in a relationship.

One can ask themselves what is the difference between understanding what you doing with regard to true love, or to acknowledge having failed to find yourself in this way of life. Love is when you understand that a break up is not the end of the world, and making sure that whatever happens you do not let circumstances change you. Regardless of what you go through, within a certain period of separation, you come out of it the way you are, and you're able to do things right.

Along the way you could have become important to yourself, and you have find the center in everything that you do, and somehow true love comes knocking in your heart. Yet you not sure of whether is commitment and you are not willing to give in with your whole heart, as you fear being broken, however, you mustn't be scared of such a situation. If someone lets you down, life will pick you up and put you right back at your place, where you belong, as you are of love, you deserve being given the best out of all that exists.

We owe it to this life to love with all that we have, without holding anything back, it pleases some entity within us to give ourselves to the other completely. Is more of an obligation that we have, to surrender who we are, with no questions or whatsoever, part of the world is dependent on us to commit to each other.

Is like a sacred entity, a journey, or a purpose that we serve towards creation, we are somehow compensated for everything that we give. We are reimbursed for loving one another honestly, and if you can observe very well in creation you will understand that it is important to carry that virtue, as it is rare to find in human lives.

People cannot come into your life to hurt you all the time, there will be a period where you will be vulnerable, and during that time is where you must be very careful about a lot that you allow into your heart. It could also be about anything that you value, and someone wanted to drop you for it, if you have love in your heart, for whatever they could have wanted to disappoint you for, and depending on how far they could have wanted you to go down.

True love will still catch you, as far as you had been dropped, and sometimes when situations catches you, be able to come back with a strong foundation. So that when someone wants to let you down again, you always fall within your comfort, given that it will be everything against the person that you are forever.

You will be hunted by so much, and it will always want to begin something that could have come to an end. Situations always challenges someone to weaken them more and more, given that there is another place where you might fall in to. For a woman you can lose hope and become anything, like a prostitute, and for a man you can resent to anything that you know is not you. It could be liquor, or any other substances, in reality you're being pulled to pass that level whereby a responsible human being must remain at.

You must choose the kind of a person that you want to become, knowing that the world can consume you, and that you can kiss the good life goodbye, if you lack faith and hope in love. So much continues to question our intentions, do you forever believe in relationships, time after time, how do you keep falling for someone, when you know that commitment hurts? When do you admit that something is wrong deep within your heart, and when does it matter to the people that we are, to accept the truth, that a lot is not right and has now become a burden to carry?

Is when someone get to that place where I was, to be completely left alone, and abandoned by everything, including love. Only that I had begun to understand so much that it didn't matter what had happened in the past, what mattered is that from what I knew now I was moving on to a better direction.

It was a hopeless situation and hurting deeply from lacking true love, that it has affected your entire being, you know that you can break out, but not when you want to. Meanwhile to recover from such a setback you will have to sacrifice a lot, and so many people will come to pass, and they would've been very important in making life a pleasure to enjoy.

Some of these people had been my ideal description of a good partner, yet they don't describe what I was permanently looking for in someone to spend the rest of my life with. You learn to let go of such human beings, though they would've played significant roles in making so much feel easy, and you continue to value them for the part they would've represented on your daily basis.

It is love that can create a lot of pain in our hearts, when we have to allow that nature of individuals to pass. Although at times we can try to justify it with lacking necessities to be able to settle down. Part of you feels at ease knowing that there's this place that exists in spirit, where true love will find you at the right time.

You acknowledge that you can only survive through love, yet things would make that much sense when everything is complete. For true love is calm, and mostly honored by our efforts and achievements, and heading towards a good direction of life, and it is only through that dedication that you will be reunited with whatever you seek and the one you desire most.

You can go all over the world searching for answers to whatever it is that you truly seek with your whole heart, and when you reach the end. You get to understand that you could be looking for something that might be the only thing you need to reach success. It is a place that defines all your true desires through your knowledge, and mostly how to really love a person, and it will not offer the solution to that only, but also help you to know things better than you did before.

People who fail to arrive at this level of understanding are likely to develop a sense of dependency, and someone can lose so much when their well-being depends on other's capabilities. Especially when one has failed to remain true in loving the other, or finding a solution to something that can help them rectify the wrongs they've committed.

Here at the center, is a place for those who have dedicated themselves in delivering quality of the heart, a lot who dwell here understand the value of loving a person completely. They continue to seek for love even when situations don't allow them to, as they acknowledge that nothing can ever rectify being alone.

The strange thing about the pain that we feel deep in our hearts, is that at times is not caused by the people we seek to love. It comes from so much that we need to achieve which we mostly find ourselves lacking the direction to reach for. You become disturbed by something that you truly desire, as the way becomes hard to move on, everything just leads one to feeling dropped and forsaken.

As if having a need out of the ordinary, has become a huge weakness that one has adopted, however, from deep within and honestly living our lives, all that we do serves the purpose of true love. Even though a lot that we do doesn't fit the goal we have to find someone that we truly care for, and it brings a lot of confusion when one cannot easily reach for that special person, as the path to that place is through greater achievements. Yes we can't have it all, only that the life we live and the desires we have could be the only way to be accepted by the kind of human beings that we seek.

You could have chosen to follow the route of love as a way to greater understanding, yet you must acknowledge the fact that, alone is not enough, we need all that we are in order to achieve satisfaction from life. Though some are fully dedicated to caring about the other, and have committed their entire lives to loving that special person only. Like a fully committed Christian marriage is not the same to what we settled for, yes is true love as well, only that it became what it is somewhere else, not before the eyes of Christians.

You can't be blamed for wanting more than just a good relationship, is what life is, I didn't want to ever change, I wanted to remain this person that I am, I couldn't live to regret what I could have been, if I was to give up on this way of doing things. Everything here at the center is about cycling what we have discovered as love within us, we allow the passion for our work to be what drives or leads the way forward.

You live with confidence knowing that you have discovered a special kind of gift which is rare to find in an ordinary world, and it gives you the light to avoid disappointing surprises as you move through. You become so bold when you know that you've prepared yourself for all the challenges that one can face in a lifetime.

As you prepare for the rest of your life, love was among the most important weapons that you needed to have. Yet you don't know all the time what you preparing yourself for, you're getting ready for one of the greatest adventures on earth. True love was not how we have planned to live our lives completely, it became somewhat the most necessary thing that we were required to have, to see through situations with ease.

At times I felt it being the most difficult thing to ever achieve, given the fact that you have to be patient about everything that you doing, if you are to find the love that you seek. Challenges keeps emerging as you search for that quality of life in a human being, and a lot becomes very hard to deal with. You arrive where you get to understand that the nature of what you looking for comprises of so much, and it will take more than just the will to witness that being a reality.

You traveling ahead feeling lost as you don't know what you doing and where you headed, to move forward becomes very hard and difficult to understand. Yet if you ever get there or see the results of what you've created, you become very amazed at the wonder of life, and the beauty of the world you have brought to existence.

That is the cornerstone of the kind of understanding that wouldn't be easy to achieve, which I had struggled to build on my own. That I would live to know that whenever life becomes a deficiency, then love drops, as human beings can become subject to situations and they can act upon their own will, yet someone would be there to catch me. I could say that if things were ever difficult, that is how I would want so much to have happened, as a lot can be given, only that with some of our desires we work hard for. You don't know what founds you, still, even when there was no foundation, love did know how to keep you from falling.

It is very important for one seeking a path through true love to have that undying faith in it, as it does know how to defend us from everything that can ever happen or try to harm us, and that's how you can find peace forever. Is a very amazing feeling that you can get as someone who has dedicated their lives to something they desire, and achieving what they wanted at the end, to arrive where you live without fear as a result of whatever you needed to succeed. A goal that allows you to be exactly what you longed for, a place where you can give everything that you are to love, with no fear, or any need to hold back.

Chapter Twelve

Love is deep

Happiness is about how we find value from what we have, especially from how much something really matters in someone's daily life. With regard to the fact that we only get one opportunity to share a very special moment with each other. Love is like always saying goodbye, sometimes we can miss the greatest moment of our lives by a minute. You just allow your partner to walk out of the house, little did you know that person was leaving you forever. You can try to bring him or her back, only that they're nowhere to be found, they have left you permanently.

You could be making love to each other, and say "let's take a break", whereas you will never have that opportunity to share on that special moment again. No matter what you do to get another chance, it becomes difficult and impossible, and you have walked out of one another's life forever. Who have we allowed to walk away from us, just before we can tell them how important and precious they are? At times we fail to recognize how significant it is to resemble care for our partner's every day. You have that opportunity to tell your lover that "I love you" right now, and do everything that you need to do together and be happy.

So that you can be satisfied with how you attempted to fulfill your obligations, you tried to maintain love and caring for each other, that can in turn give you some closure. You can find peace, from that unlikely event of walking away from someone, or the other deserting you forever. Yet I refuse to associate that with dying, death is a loss, love is emptiness, loneliness, emotional stress, it belongs in its own world.

The way relationships are meant to be is that you have to try with your whole heart to focus your attention on caring about one another. Even if not all the time, but once in a lifetime be focused on resembling true love for your partner, the way it is required of you. It can be a very difficult experience to deal with after one has walked out of your life, as some can only realize the value of a commitment when someone has already left their presence. Given that we tend to be ignorant of certain things which are the most important to look out for in relationships or when loving each other.

Most especially for some man, being involved in caring for their partners honestly, is only meant for a specific period of time, as sooner or later they lose focus on true love. They get satisfaction too early in a relationship, yet women tend to be focused on everything that there is around them, and they make use of every opportunity there is available to love the other wholeheartedly.

Being committed to someone requires one to pay attention to what could be the most important thing to make one another happy. Do not be blindfolded by situations or let that opportunity passes you, as you lack care for your lover. This could apply to every stage of a communion, don't let it grow old, remain young, active, and ambitious about pleasing each other.

You allowed that person whom you care so much for to walk out of your life or home as if you know what the future holds. Unfortunately we are not the only ones who exist out there, and the world wouldn't stop living as we want to have things our way. You don't know what might come in between two people in love, or what could accidentally hurt a human being, or maybe convince them otherwise.

Never allow anyone that you love to walk out of the house sad, they might find someone to comfort them, or they could console themselves with something else. Fulfill the objectives of a relationship to keep each other happy at all times, let it be an obligation towards pleasing and living happily with one another.

The thing that you'll come across is that you can try to fix it in the future, yet you would have spent time alone. You might find another one, but is not the same person, and people cannot be repeated, they only came once. Mostly when trouble comes in between you, the question that follows is, how long will it take you to reach for true love again?

True love does exist, you know you miss that unique individual that cared for you deeply, the only person who has ever loved you honestly, and completely gave themselves to you. At times we get used to living with someone, and they become part of our lives and everything we have ever needed in a human being.

You don't just put everything behind, and open your heart to a complete stranger, thinking that you will be happy overnight, how can someone just replace all the good times we had with each other? That's the value of the love we shared together, deep down inside there is still so much that we've exchanged, things you cannot understand how crucial they are in bringing a commitment to reality. The strength it takes to build a relationship, a home, a family, there's just nothing to live for outside that area where you've invested your entire life.

I looked outside and wondered what have I done for me to be alone like this? Yet it was all there, everything you can ever need in a human being, or desire in a lifetime. You could even wish that when in a relationship, you need to take a break, do you really have to stop even just for a single day? You are together, yes you might need to focus on something else, but not that you could do it apart from each other. However, you decide to stay out there, thinking that you will breakthrough it on your own, and you knew that is wrong about love.

You throwing so much away, the connection that we've developed overtime, the daily lovemaking, after a very long time. It has this spiritual bond that has birthed so much between two people that are truly committed to one another. Trying to break away from that is to be completely lost, the way you can wonder in the world making love to someone, only to somehow appear where you know what you doing through that devotion. Relationships can form you in a way that you can never understand, you can be formed beautifully by being devoted to one person.

We can make each other in the image of the union that we have, you can walk out of here formed by the love that we share. Now when you want to break apart from that, can you really let everything go, and start all over again? Do you have the courage to put whatever we did behind, and never look back, like you saying that is over? Are you strong enough to survive another man or woman, can you open up to someone else the way you did before?

True love, can it be found, once lost? What does it mean against our differences? That place where we've been making love every day is now spiritually formed by the energy that we exchange, and the effect it will have on both of us. So if we were to walk away from one another, can it be possible elsewhere?

We can try to pretend like it doesn't exist, yet it does, it makes you forget who you are, to surrender our bodies and give in to each other every day. Can be seen as a very easy thing to do when we looking at things, without understanding the value of what we have. When is it necessary to fight for the love we have with our whole hearts, how do you know that you've given this person everything that you are, and whatever you have now is worth fighting for?

Do you care about one another that you can't let go of what you have, and no matter what you do, is for you to give in to each other more? How would you fight for someone when you don't know what it is that they engage in when they're outside, and how would you know that they will be doing everything that they need to, for you to love them more?

Love is what you can't give to yourself, something that you not, is when you see a particular entity that exist in a different world with you, and you begin to develop a certain feeling of liking so much. Is when you yearn for a thing, and you just look at it or that person, and your heart dissolves with appreciation, you welcome the difference that the other or what it resembles.

That is the foundation of love, and when you choose one among so many it is true love, and you have offered exactly what was required of a person. You have given more than what was needed from someone, we're always that much in the giving of our hearts, you yearned for what wasn't there, into your life, and made it part of who you are.

What opens up the way for the people that we are, is when we learn to appreciate the difference, and not to victimize it. Cherish the opposite, accept all, even what you don't understand about the other, don't be offensive, but rather welcome it into your life. Love is beauty, don't let it pass before you realize how important it is, to an extent that you must not let anything or anyone steal the tenderness that you have in your heart. No matter how difficult it can be, don't lose hope, care to the end of your lives, until there's nothing left, better to have tried than to just throw everything away like that.

Sometimes it becomes difficult to understand that you must let someone go, accept the differences that have emerged between the two of you. Instead of torturing yourself with something, that you know very well does not exist anymore, love doesn't have to be a pain that you carry in your heart. Yet you can live with knowing that you're better off alone for some time, if whatever you've engaged in, no longer serves your intention.

To care about the other so much doesn't mean that you're fragile, you must be tough in relationships, and when it comes to dealing with issues in that area of your life. You must be able to handle your affairs, with dignity, pride, and integrity, stand strong on your ground by being honest of what you really need.

At times love can disappear between two people that have shared so much together, from whatever it is that could have gone wrong, and then after a while, you have to learn to live with all that has come to pass. It could've happened somewhere so deep that you cannot forget how things used to be, and somehow you cannot put behind what you've been through, and regrets follow.

"Only if I had learned to measure the other's commitment in the relationship, before I gave my whole heart completely, maybe I would've been safe." Then you ask yourself, how will I sustain myself over a period of loneliness, or just to clearly remember who I was, and what I've been doing before I met this person?

One does need to be alone to have closure and comfort from all the love that you've lost, learning to be a human being apart from someone. Even if it wasn't a serious relationship, once you are in it, and there are activities between you, whatever you feel for each other, can take away something in your heart, it can weaken you emotionally.

For a very long time I felt lost, but regardless of that, somehow I knew that I was always after something that really mattered to my inner happiness, and very genuine to my heart's joy. Constantly without expectation something else would happen, just to ruin the spark of love. It could be a period where things haven't worked out your way, even if you try to engage with someone you can hurt yourself or those around you. When you look at things the best solution is being alone for some time, give it a break, maybe the world will once again forgive you and answer your prayers to have a committed individual.

We do get to a point whereby life has marked us invalid, especially when you had been deeply involved with someone before. Woman mostly have this tendency of measuring time for man, to think carefully about their decision, and one can remain there in spirit, searching for all the love that there is, only to find that there is none.

About when to engage in a relationship after a break up? You must always be alert, there could be times where you know things can never work your way, and you have to wait. The thing is not everyone that comes into our lives is worth committing to, so do not just look for anyone, try to find someone who is truly honest and worthy of being committed to, a person who is very motivating.

You don't have to chase after love, especially when you haven't understood clearly with whom you should be in a communion with. You will meet a worthwhile individual at some point, without expecting how it came about. As long as you live with a strong will to achieve true happiness, it will happen at the end, and you will be happy forever.

Some issues can at times make love hard and difficult to understand, it could be that you are not where you're supposed to be. Given the fact that people sometimes respond to different circumstances in life. With all the complications that relationships have to deal with, having to go through a situation where you find someone who is single, it is not easy.

It is highly unlikely to find a person who is not involved with anyone, people have commitments. Hence we say that for a man and woman living with a purpose is better to stay in love, loving each other truly. It could help to clearly have a better perspective on what you want to achieve. If you failing to maintain the balance in that area of our lives, you might begin to see yourself becoming less important to who you are, and having to put up with that, could turn to be a very embarrassing outcome in one's journey.

Even if you were to master a certain way of life, yet there's where you have to prove your worth, you must be able to deeply focus on love if you are to see good results. When standing at a distance, you're being given a chance to work your way back to each other's arms. However, when you get next to one another, is now time to show how much you've learned about true love and caring for the other completely. You can't deny yourself an opportunity to please your partner once you've come to understand that there is getting closer to someone with a purpose to resemble utmost care.

It comes down to that period when you get closer to each other that you have to fulfill your objectives as individuals that longs to be happy. You need to play your part in every learning curve in a relationship. You will find time to test how well you've understood what is required of you, and then you have to make use of all the chance you get to please one another.

Do not be selfish, and let things be about yourself alone, think about your partner and the love you need in your life, and be true to that. True love is the period when you cannot see one another, and be able to sustain yourselves over that time frame. Then you're able to work your way back to each other's arms as soon as possible, you don't allow anything to come between you forever.

A relationship should be able to satisfy both of you and create hunger for the other when you're not around each other. It must produce a feeling of wanting to be together so much, and be fully convinced is how things must be, and that is for all of you to be completely happy. Do not underestimate the quality of the attention you suppose to give to one another, you need to give love a special care.

At some point I thought that a woman would just be interested in loving me without a reason, but no, when you learn to focus deeply on a relationship that you happy about, you get to understand that you need to fulfill your duties. See love uniting your hearts in a way that you just want to be together forever, and you're strong for it, and keen on showing each other how much you live to witness the others desires being fulfilled.

Do not lose focus on what truly matters in the union of hearts, you don't need to bring extra energy from outside the relationship. Everything about love, is when you care so much about this special person, and you never get bored of each other. You work hard every day by all means possible to close the gap that could want to exist between you, and when that happens you have arrived at that place called true love. Deepened the attention you give to your communion, and share your joyful presence with one another. You will be surprised because a true commitment has more power and so much to give than you can ever imagine.

Is all there, all you need to do is to pay attention, and focus on what needs to be done carefully. No one can ever find a space to come in between lovers, when they're both present, with the intention of falling deeper with one another. The more you give to each other, you pushing the negative energy out of your lives, destroying whatever could want to exist, and see love being given its place to crown.

I will not ever forget how wonderful it is to think that you're serving a special purpose being alone, only that you've brought that to yourself. Is when you've failed in a relationship, where you can try something else until you are ready for commitment again, Understand everything that love requires, and give it another chance, with someone special to see if you can succeed this time.

Value the opportunity you have to be with your partner and make use of that time wisely. How deep is love? Love is deep, and continues to be deepened by the attention we give to each other, and it is the most necessary thing to do. You can regret not ever doing so much right, and you could be punished severely for all that you've neglected. Every relationship has a heartbeat, and is alive like any living object, and very powerful, so always try to deal with things from a point of respect.

You cannot fool anyone where love is the concern, by being negligent in a relationship you only fooling yourself, you need to understand very well how to handle the nature of this affairs, everything to care for is always happening around us. So respect the laws that you learn about commitments, and take an ought that you will forever follow them accurately.

Being committed to someone is no foolish game, we all learn as we go on, and that can never be a lesson you learned on your first day. We gain the necessary experience in the path that we traveling, it is very important to acquire the required knowledge in this regard. As relationships can be too tiring in the earliest stages, however, you can apply patience, endurance, and perseverance until you find that hold on everything happening around your lives, and be able to move forward clearly.

Is not like a childhood fantasy, where a girl meets a boy, hold hands, and living happily ever after. Growth has commitments and that might need you to wait until those premature stages have passed, and maybe you can find a place in that person's heart.

Part Three

Part Three

Island in the Sea

You could be in a relationship with someone to fulfill your personal reason, yet life can end up discovering your true purpose, on whether you're in it for love, or you just enjoy being with a person for you to ruin their lives, or to benefit out of it. Creation has a way of uncovering our real intentions about everything that we engage in, you can say or do whatever you want. Only that deep within you know the truth, your ultimate objectives, why you doing what it is that you feel necessary.

Are we dedicated to each other as much as we use to, have you in some way questioned the validity of what you doing, or why the need to do it? That's the most important thing about relationships, you don't have to hide your true intentions or stop along the way and ask yourself, why am I still involved with this person?

Relationships are one thing set apart from the rest, you have to find a way to understand how things work around it, is our fair share of life. Nobody is unworthy or undeserving of true love, it is a simple way for everyone to find comfort. You don't have to doubt the love that you have in your heart, you too deserve someone special to commit to you, and regardless of whatever it is you could have given yourself to. So if you have faith in what you have committed your life to, you will meet a person worthy of who you are.

One needs to be very courageous in committing themselves, always give yourself without a doubt or questions of what could go wrong. Although you may want to know how committed the other is, you mustn't lose sight on fulfilling the obligations that you have towards each other. As it does happen that life might turn out to be overwhelming, that you don't recognize how important and precious your lover is.

In the right sense is always safe to love, knowing that you trust your judgment, given that you could make that mistake, of misusing the confidence that someone has on you, only to realize later that they're worth everything after you've lost them.

Understanding the values of an honest relationship is to be true to yourself and your lover, and by being faithful, we giving ourselves entirely in loving one another. That kind of dedication measures our devotion towards each other, you don't have to take back your love from the one who has accepted you, for who you are, and what you've turn out to be.

There's a way in which everything became what it is today, we were all loved to life, so when you stop living the way you came to be a human, you're not fair to creation. Yes we sometimes overlook how we were created as a result of being young and ambitious, and we no longer care about our essence, and because of that, we left so much behind, of which must be considered very well.

Is not that we're unable to understand how to love each other honestly, is how we lack character in taking things serious from an early age. Now life has reached the end where so much must be valued in essence, our every move, mistakes, or inability to reflect seriousness, has now become an issue that could stand in our way. Everything that we do as we grow up, while lacking the power of understanding, and consideration, can harm you deeply, as it serves a significant purpose. When you not thinking about how important this time that you have is, you fail to recognize how lucky you are in a situation.

This issues that we overlook somehow become real life obstacles, at the end we lose our way towards our destiny. We not who we are because we chose to be that, we are sometimes changed by circumstances and the situations that we go through. The need to follow our heart, where we foresee happiness, is where we go. You can begin a certain path of creativity knowing very well what you doing, yet the outcome turns you into something that you didn't choose to be.

Is what the universe made of the person that you were, you're at the final stage, and you are no longer what you use to be. If that's not enough, is that I am a very good individual, and we at times do things not knowing how the outcome will be, or maybe make a mistake without an idea what impact that will have on your daily well-being.

After a while that has passed and I didn't die from what I became, what am I supposed to do with myself? As I still have a life to cherish, and if I didn't decease from what I encountered, then I might as well keep on living. I wouldn't stop existing from what I went through, and you might forget about what happened and begin to live to your fullest capabilities. Yet that as well at the end changes the outcome of so much and the shape of reality as we have known things.

Though sometimes it feels wrong to manipulate situations to your advantage, the fact that you still a human, gives you the right to want everything out of life, including love. To so many it will be as if is a wrong thing to do, even if something bad happened to you, it doesn't seem well to capitalize on things knowing it might ruin people's lives.

Yes it could be an unusual experience that you encountered, yet one needs to understand that we all go through the same trials, and is true we are made different by these tests that we face. There's nothing that someone can endure which another hasn't endured on their own. Everyone began at that place, living for that particular thing that everybody wants, and we still long for similar things out of this world, we only became differentiated from the desire that we have.

The goal that we seek to manifest in the world is what becomes the drive towards that place which is the center for all that we want, and if you persistent enough, you become the magnet pulling whoever seeks to follow a similar path. Through faith in what you have turn out to be, everything of who you are is treasured as you are not afraid to resemble your true self.

For some our work of creativity becomes the magnet and the shield from everything out there, as at times it becomes necessary for one to be protected by their higher self. The love we have for what we're dedicated to, protects us from all that could want to harm us. Our hearts are meant to perform the functions of who we are, and what we do, against the people who don't deserve our goodness, and what we are.

True love is our determination to transform our own lives, we become the slaves of our goals, is when you strive to see exactly what you doing, and you pull the same from the outside world. You begin to experience everything that you value coming back to life, and it must be able to attract only what is worthy of you.

As one needs to understand that you can be easily attacked by people, or situations unworthy of what you've striven to accumulate. Given the fact that you have no idea of what someone was doing yesterday, and when you meet with that person, you know nothing about who they are, and what they've done so far, you just get taken away, as no one has a proof of who we are.

Now that I've been innocent my whole life, who speaks for me in that kind of situation, who knows what I deserve, how can I get justice for what I am? Whatever we dedicate ourselves to accomplish with our whole hearts, becomes our higher perfection. You can work your entire life, while thinking that nobody cares about what you do, at the end you will find the reward for all that you did.

The same could apply to relationships, you could have planted your seed of love, and someone just come and pluck it out, or robs you of your kind heart, if true love isn't there to protect you. Now your seeds never became fruitful, all that you've ever valued has disappeared, and you will not ever witness the results of it again.

So much could be said about being persistent in terms of seeking your true desires, or finding a worthwhile relationship as well. How it all brings joy into a man and a woman's heart at the end, I still believe that if we never give up, we do find our answers. Although are some words that we got used to, and maybe they could have lost meaning.

Yet they mean exactly what you will understand when you get to the finishing line of every project, or a journey, that you got whatever you wanted. How time played a very important role in making sure that everything became what you desired when it was still valid. How would you justify the life that you've lived only to be robbed by circumstances or unworthy situations? It would mean that the world isn't a fair platform for creativity and love.

Some things you will never believe they do have an end, because of how they can insist on taking a very long time to become a reality, and you might think of quitting from the pain you feel trying to see what you want, or something come to being. However, if you are patient, whatever idea you have, will make sense at some point, and you look at a new chapter, or the beginning of a different path that leads to greener pastures.

The minute you reach the final stage, so much is meant to become real, there's a lot that begins to manifest when you have completed a certain journey, there's beauty to live for. Is all in the road that you traveling, everything that could have been a problem becomes easy to understand. Is just that when you busy fighting each other for the same thing you can never see the results thereof.

When you searching for answers to something which only you knows what it could be, sometimes the way to the end can be very strange. Somehow you might be surprised at the wonder of how long this journey, can take a human being to travel to that place where you begin to understand.

Then you start to realize that there's no need to fight with human beings when you can't see what you doing, as you lack motivation and patience, while all that is important is completing the journey. If you not courageous enough to witness your ideas become a reality, you can always settle for less and have whatever is available, that's all there is when you not strong enough to build your own life.

As we insist on doing what we care about most, along the way we do become what we really desire, and you will find the love that you deserve. Nothing is meant to hold us back forever, or take the goodness we have in our hearts away from us. It becomes beautiful when you are done with everything, as you witness your knowledge being cycled by creativity and transform your understanding into reality.

You could've been praying for a very long time, and you want your faith to become a living testimony, and you have that as your only way to life, and there's nothing else that you know or understand. Deep within you it exists that you cannot go back, as there wouldn't be anything you would rather be, only that you mustn't lose hope. One day the world will hear you clearly and answers your prayers in a way that will come to surprise you and everyone around you.

Unlike with scientific experiments where projects have time frames, you need to be patient only for a specific period, and if nothing happens, you begin to question yourself whether you're right or wrong. Maybe your understanding or calculations are incorrect, yet there's no need to go back to that point before you started working. From what you've done you could've gain enough knowledge to witness a new reality come to be.

They say that we don't resemble true love, yet we've passed a lot of stages to go back to where we started. We began from nothing, and these levels that we've gone through became our point of transformation, and that should be recognized as love for all that we are. So with every journey to understanding, we come to experience a new beginning, only that it begins to make sense when we've advance to the next chapter and everything has been well studied, and clearly understood. Therefore by continuously completing one task after another, we become formed by true devotion and dedication, and that can be used to create a destiny worth living for.

It is always important that you must sustain your mind through these tests of life, to witness precisely what you have been doing. Although you might go through jealousy as you live to transform yourself through knowledge and understanding. At the end you will be called devoted, given that you've resembled faith and you were able to go pass everything and you brought back positive results.

The person that you are must truly believe in the idea that has founded your perception. When you are a normal human being, within you have that sense of the world that exists, that is rooted deep in your soul, and eventually forms your beliefs. For someone to change you, they must dig deeper to that level where they can be able to alter whatever it is that formed your believes.

Even if is just to stray your attention from the path that you've chosen, one must strive to reach where we cycle all that we are with love, However, is not likely for one to arrive at those regions which forms the life of those who have chosen to make so much worthy happens, or without changing themselves.

The world will seek to impose on your life, change your way of doing things, by changing your beliefs in all that you doing. Yet if it's not what you are, if you couldn't see it, or if it wasn't true about who you are, then it wouldn't have built your faith and perception, or paved your way to a greater destiny.

There are things that you know we can't change about the past, yet there are those that you can see are being done intentionally with the aim of hurting humanity. One could have done some pretty bad stuff on purpose or accidentally, then along the way you realize an opportunity to use that against a lot of human beings around you. For some reason you become so eager to see people who live well or maybe those who love each other, suffering or living separate lives, for you it feels so good to dedicate your daily life just to achieve that.

Makes one wonder what is the significant of that, the need to exist with no good will for others, to hate human beings who have love for each other, what could a person be hoping to benefit from that? Being so eager to see people living separate lives, you would do anything just to achieve that. Could it be that for someone to fail finding a worthwhile relationship we are all to blame, how do you pass such an individual or avoid that kind of a situation? It happens that things would have been what they were meant to be, yet somehow anyone can learn to influence so much about the reality of those who live to love one another.

The questions that might likely follow is, how does a person learn to influence situations especially for something as good as love? To hate seeing people care for each other, the more you see them, the weaker it makes you feel, it has become part of your objectives to distract relationships. You have created ways that feed on the feelings human beings have for one another, your goal is to develop weaknesses where true love is the concerned.

You make it so hard for human beings to even be normally involved with each other. You are standing at the center of their lives awaiting every opportunity that arises so that you can ruin their chances of happiness. At the end your world has become dependent on hatred for those who love, you wish to see them deceiving one another.

That is something people can never be able to live with, to just make one mistake, and now their eligible to being separated, as their forced to lack faith and trust in each other. This represents the malfunctioning of the projects and businesses we human beings engage in, how we fail to do things well, when you get to the end you mastered the outcome, but failed to understand humanity's need for love. The rest is just meant for so many not to ever find true love for one another.

You invent things that changes you into someone so weak as a good person, and only deception strengthens your spirit. You turn your life into something that seeks to ruin the good in people, yet when you've arrive here at the center. You never make that kind of error, you understand that true love is the heartbeat of humanity and every relationship.

You must commit knowing that your life depends on it, while doing everything that needs to be done to prove your love for one another. You can never know or predict why you have to stick closer to your lover, and why you must be able to sustain yourself through every test that the world throws at you. Living with no need to even try or question what you feeling, you feel safe as you are naturally made to give what you are honestly. Not even a person whose heart is not willing or ready for commitment can ever come closer to you, from deep within you are protected by true love.

You could have discovered how to love your own way, it doesn't have to be something you learned through a religious belief. You might just be somebody who does everything that they passionate about the way it must be done, and completely devoted to seeing love being the only thing that controls your path towards life.

We don't just keep the value of love so that we can exchange it for whatever comes our way, at times you want to associate that with loving someone special, yet it can be both ways. You can do that for yourself as an individual as well, it could be anything or anyone who wants to ruin something that you hold close to your heart, and this person keeps dragging you into the dark. Only that if you've find that value in your own life, you are able to see or understand where to draw the line.

Otherwise you can let your good heart be taken away forever, or you can do something about it, you can have no shame into this human being that you are, and dedicate all your life goals to love, peace, and everlasting happiness. You are just trying to save yourself from everything which could want to ruin your life permanently, or anything that could seek to turn your purpose into a meaningless pursuit.

There is so much that exists out there that keeps fighting the love we have, to survive you must have chosen something that you really care about so much. Though you might have been lost, however, it is never too late to learn something new about creation. Part of which you can appreciate about yourself, you can have a proper life that you can enjoy as an individual. By better understanding who you are, you can unlock the doors that leads to overflowing abundance, or you can fail to see and open the gates to your deepest fears and weaknesses, how all that can aim at your heart.

I had understood so much, only that somehow I had learned to stay away from it all, for the sake of true love and happiness at the end. You have to understand how to look the opposite direction from everything out there, what if your whole life depended on you to do the right thing. You must be aware of a lot knowing that whatever you doing now, prepares you for the person that you want to be.

We live to appreciate the future of who we are, if not aiming at that part of your goals, then you could have achieved all your desires, or whatever you doing is pointless. As we only have that as our main priority, and you hold the keys to seeing some good being done, and achieved. Yet you need to be careful of so much that comes in your life, as the key also leads to your heart, and your most precious position, and if you careless it can fell in the wrong hands, however, you can take charge of everything you live for.

You can focus on the crucial parts of your well-being, your relationship, and goals can be under your control. So do not allow anything to creep into your heart and steal the tenderness you have towards your desires, you mustn't let situations control your fate. Do all that you care about in good faith, knowing that you hold greatness inside, as you are aware of what your life has for you at the end.

When lost in a maze, everything defines different characters, but not the ones that we are, we have no identities to define ourselves with. True definition comes with reaching for your ambitions and loving the person that you are. At some point I had no objective to any goal, and so I had not begun to live, as it is evident that life is better understood physically, when everything is clear to see. Then I discovered a purpose only that is still the same, when all your goals haven't been achieved, your world hasn't started to create.

You must have faith that you will pass that situation that you came across, the present prepares you for the future, and you work very hard at it knowing that you can have a great life that you choose to live. The time in which you can make a difference is today, the day that has denied you nothing. However, given you greatness in everything you want to reach for, and from that you can find your way around being the best in your personal goals and relationships.

Chapter Thirteen

Test of Life

Our minds don't operate the same as humanity, some know how to control their own way of thinking, while others don't. There are situations which you just need to analyze, and understand them, so that you can be able to pass through whatever setback you facing. I had dedicated myself deep into studying the value of things, and what creates the difference between us humans, and when does one actually matter?

What you think of all the time, can it be done, maybe someone can do it, so how about you, are you really capable of everything that you desire? Given that so much that we are as human beings means a lot to us, and the kind of people we want to permanently become.

There are a lot of people who don't see the world in the same way as you, some want to hold you back in terms of life, while others are after the love you have in your heart. Whereas it's all there to disturb you, from the way you wanted to spend every day being a happy person, living, and enjoying the pleasures of this universe with someone that you care for so much.

You find your faith put to the test, and you begin to observe sideways, trying to resent to things which you know very well cannot help you, and part of it will only come to destroy the person that you are. In your heart you are fully aware that you're responsible for choosing whom you want to become in the future. Your whole life spent without responsibilities, or you can take control of what you eager to be, which you positive that you can.

To be held back in love, all against the person that you long to be with, someone that you wanted to share more than just quality time together, the only one you dreamed of spending every day closer to. Only that people are pulling you to different directions, however, for now you're stuck, and without a clue on what to do.

I had been living this life, and learning so much about the world that could turn me into a good person, mostly in understanding. One who knows how to handle his personal affairs, and with a space reserved for love. So many times I questioned myself, do I focus on doing my own thing because of being capable of reaching for success, or is it that deep in me I have true love, and eager to spend quality time with someone special? Or maybe I had imagine everything being good at the end, yet so much can come in between human beings, and steal away that tenderness for all that they want.

So it became the sort of a path where I had found myself traveling in vain, and mostly doing things alone, and somehow it seems like everything that you engage in is not important any more. That's how you feel when you look at situations, or you could give yourself a little longer, or maybe more to it, so that you can get things right?

True love is the ultimate conqueror, yet at times it does go through difficult stages, and when you want to resolve all the difficulties that you encounter, and find your way back to someone's arms. Only to learn that situations could be harder than you think, and no matter what you do, there's just nothing that you can change at a glance. You try to fix it and things become more than you can handle, sometimes we're tested on every level, even when is not necessary, but if love was really true and all that exists out there is just false illusion, You know you have to work hard so that you can reach for it.

It didn't matter how long it will take, whether I go through good or bad experiences, even if it wasn't true for some time, I wanted to live the lie, wherever it gets me, it would be enough. When does it ever become love, or how long does it take to be true love? Or maybe when we both are willing to fight the world for everything that we need and deserve.

Maybe you don't have to go through as much trouble as there is, somehow life can be lived in a very simple manner. At times it feels like we're the only one who wanted everything out of this world, and the rest don't seem to care, hence the difficulties that we face. How do you hope to achieve all that you want, when so much keeps on moving in its own direction? So can you really handle the pressure when you get to see that things are not only about you, and how will you influence situations for your desires to come to you, or let alone travel along with you?

Do you feel great about what you so eager to achieve that you would sacrifice everything that you know for it to become a reality? And when is it necessary for someone to actually do what they must, to have what they desire? You go through so much knowing that all you ever wanted was just love, yet it comes with responsibilities, and you need to have done everything or worked very hard to find it where is true. Does it matter how long it will take to have that, or what matters is that you will finally get it, and you will forever be grateful for that opportunity, as you would've got your fair share of life.

If you want something genuine and worthwhile, you must learn to distinguish yourself from the rest of the people who exists out there. A path chosen to fulfill both your physical and spiritual needs, and be sure that whatever happens you don't ever go back.

When is really true love that motivated you from deep within, and truly the purpose you've been carrying throughout your entire life, you need to keep moving forward. Though you could be required to carry it to the end, as it is worth everything that you can ever imagine. Regardless of the fact that you might regret some things or stare at the world feeling lost, but fear not, for it will be fulfilled, and why wouldn't you have it if you want it with your whole heart.

Does it feel impossible to achieve your desires, now that you've begun the search for it, "and how did so much become a secret until you began traveling your own path? And somehow discovering later that your way is not the only one that leads to success, others have their routes as well, it might not make any sense to you, given that everyone lives their respective life. If that was not the case, how would things had been, would it be that the world had been very boring and predictable? Or is just circumstances and situations the way they are.

As difficult as things may be, we still want to carry our desires through, our ambitions for greatness and love, that's all we've ever needed, life the way it is. Yet growth has taken its toll, and now the world is very demanding, so much is not the way we had predicted it to be. You want to grow into everything that you had been hoping to achieve, however, there's a huge mountain standing in your way.

You want to come out of it, yet you keep disappearing with all that you've started, given that you cannot go back to being the person that you were. Now you had been coming with it for a very long time, or maybe you might be lost, could you have required someone to guide, or prepare you for everything that you were to come across?

By living for your beloved ambitions seems like your being left back in so much, and how will you ever catch up on things? When is it enough to forget about what you desired, your dreams and goals, and devote all your efforts towards loving everything that is necessary for life? Not needing more out of this world, being satisfied with the little that you have, and living for what everybody cares about.

It was being a victim of circumstances, that made me feel so weak, or else I would have wanted to have what everyone wants out of this beautiful creation, and maybe settle for whoever comes my way as well. How do you suggest things be done? When you can't have what every ordinary individual has, do you give up on everything there is to live for? Or you aim higher than anyone around you, struggle with it until it begins to make sense?

Do you walk away from all there is to live for, and try to fit in the context of ordinary, whether you would've had more, less, or enough? Or maybe if there was a better way to do what we like, you continue to work hard, await that opportunity to arise, and take as much as there is to be a human being for, true love, and everything that comes with it.

The thing is that life has secret paths to success, and everyone has discovered their own, yet the question is, does it work for you? Would it be better to discover yours, or you will learn to follow someone else's way? If you choose to be a follower, are you ready to do everything there is, in order to get to the part where you achieve what you want? Given that some things are individually motivated, unlike living through the ordinary route, you just have to do what every normal person does.

You work to earn a living and love comes from that, now with all the different routes there are to more money, and abundance in everything, things are kind of unusual. So if you willing to adapt, then how much of you, or what you've known are you prepared to sacrifice, and give in to this ways? If you are to make them your life as well, do they cater for love along the way? Or you will have to wait until you reach the end so that you can find someone who cares about you, after you've achieved the best, in what you desired?

When I was not out there discovering the world, I wanted to spend every day of my life loving someone who deserves all that I am. However, now that the world we live in comes with responsibilities, if you have failed to find who you are, and what you need to be doing, everything just looks away. Given that even relationships have requirements and obligations that you need to fulfill, before you can be able to say I am settled, and happy with whoever I have come to meet as my partner.

So much could be hidden from us when love is still pure and innocent, yet if you ever break out of it, and come back again, you are likely to go through a lot of difficulties. You get to see things where it's not how you've perceived it to be, and become subject to hardships that have been invented by human beings, as relationships are no longer true like they used to be.

Sometimes you don't need all the stress, about being the best and different from the rest, things can be done easy. You can spend so much time arguing about it, and how you wanted to achieve all that you dreamed of, through your own understanding. Yet you know is true, is not like we don't get the chance to have a clear picture of what's the most important thing to have. We just demand too much out of life, and we want it when it suits us, while love was always there, and being the most necessary to have first.

If we were born with no other option except to live through this ordinary way of life, what would you want from whatever is available, or enjoy about everything a day has to offer? Remember that what you're eager to achieve now, could be against so much that as human beings we exist for, is not something given just like that. Yes it could come to be or manifest in some future, however, it will be from sacrificing yourself and working very hard to breakthrough.

When you have given all that you could and reached the end, when there's nothing left that you haven't seen or experienced, what do you want or need right now, despite everything that could come to be in the future? We wanted love, and to be close with the ones that cares about our physical or spiritual needs. We not undermining as much as there is to live for, we just have some special desire, which is to find part of who we are, to this world, our true essence.

Do we really know what we want and how to get it, and very challenging when you haven't even breakthrough to complete understanding? So many times you still find yourself standing there and wondering if what you doing aligns with what you want to see. While bearing the pain of having to do the right thing, or just to apply your knowledge correctly, and needing to have faith in something that has never been done?

Living with the eagerness to see something coming to life, so that you can live in a vision that you've created for yourself, and when it finally become true, who has any power to challenge that? I couldn't believe that you can be held captive by your own ideas, your thoughts, knowing that is difficult, but if is really what you want to witness come to existence then you must continue.

This proves that so much can be harmful if you were to give up or abandon your ideas, you can't give life to something and quit before it reaches the light. Maybe is the promises that we make to ourselves when we are at the beginning, and along the way you feel like quitting or breaking the covenant that you've made to your own creation.

Then it is the ought that you make to yourself at the foundation that determines the outcome of what you doing, and the need to remain true to them which leads to success. Obviously if you don't want to succumb your ideas must be different from a lot that exist out there. Even if is something that needs to be mastered, you have to keep going to be clearly understood by everyone, who will want to follow you.

This is another form of true love and commitment that we give to what we care about most, as we come from different backgrounds, yet we all want to see some justice to what we do. That is at the end where we deserve, as it is a life that must find its way, but what is the right approach to finding everything that we desire and love as well. Not that which everyone finds from engaging with any activity and settle, the value of working hard that brings true happiness and fulfillment when you've done things right.

When the day has turned out to be the most important to all that you've struggled for, and you have achieved whatever it is that you truly desired. You cannot be denied an opportunity to love, for what you know, with everything that life can be, you deserve what you worth.

No wonder there's a price to pay for a lot that we need, for someone that has invented their own way. How long did it take to complete everything, that you will want something from that specific outcome of their life? How do you cope with all the needs that can be denied? When you're on a journey to creativity, knowing that you cannot drink from a fountain that has been dug by another person. You have to acknowledge that you must've created whatever it is you require for yourself, if you heading your own direction.

When can we at least live love, even if is not the whole package, some part of it, we not overlooking the money and everything that comes with being human, we just want to be able to feel alive, and better? To be with someone that you care about makes you forget who you are, as we are never guilty of anything, and we don't have to be made to pay the price for what we believe in.

We just loved the universe and believed that through it we can do so much as human beings, that's if you really know what you doing and believing in whatever it is that has founded your perception, and knowing how it must come to life. You live to change the shape of reality, from how it was, you want to add an impact. From what it used to be, people are going to be made to forget about a lot that there was, and that disturbs some reality of our true values. So how long are we supposed to wait before things can go back to normal, or when will it be free to love each other again?

With all the theories that exist, what is the best that needs to be taken into account, is our love for life, against true love for each other? All depends on how you feel about whatever it is that you want to achieve. In order to have greatness out of this existence, you must have resembled some true quality in understanding. On the other hand to have someone giving themselves to you, without a doubt or hesitation needs one to deserve such warmth. So to have success in both spheres requires a lot of dedication into everything that is worth living for, and to be persistent in your quest to be outstanding.

At times the solution to succeeding in what we do should be to approach all that we engage in with love, and carrying ourselves with such dedication, and not to ever forsake that warmth for existence, as it will be what lead us to whatever it is we desire. Knowing that if you ever abandon that foundation to life you will never find it anywhere in the world, and taking it with us is our insurance towards everything that comes in our lives.

As people we do die, sometimes we can face some really deep setback and end up opting for anything that you know isn't true about ourselves. The world of human beings is capable of pulling you back from everything that matters, yet if you kept that warmth of life, you feel safe. Knowing it has driven you from too far in the past and you can use it to thrive through adversaries. As it came with you from where you had been completely lost to the day you found yourself by understanding how to use it to face reality, so you cannot live that kind of love behind.

We can live life in many ways, but which one makes sense to you, the path that you began to understand now through the love you have for the whole of existence, or going back to that way which you failed to succeed in anything as you lacked true ambitions? There is no crime that you committed in discovering your own understanding, failure belongs to the world where you escaped, back there where everything had no meaning to whatever humanity lives for.

Success can at times emerge from situations where we had lost hope in what we doing as we lack courage to understand things better, yet if you can just keep pushing and grab hold of that purpose that discovers your true intentions. You will be surprised that you will find yourself where you've been stuck forever, and unlock all the doors that leads to an everlasting abundance in whatever it is that you do.

With our own understanding comes the light, though this world is not owned by one man, and it will challenge you with all that exists, however, is where a little is worth more than you desired. Although in some situations it might be impossible to see the way, still, it would better help in finding a worthwhile relationship. The thing is that your thoughts matters the most, even if you have to go through mastering so much to understand things well. Is everything to live for at the end, regardless of how much time you can lose trying to figure things out clearly.

So much can leave you feeling weary and tired trying to understand whatever it is that exists out there. To succeed it requires one to have given themselves completely to what they love, you don't blink or look aside, and all of you must be deeply in it. You take what has been given to you and transform it into life for everyone to witness the tenderness you hold in your heart, hence we define it as true love for creativity.

There's just so much that you will need, only that it can never happen when you want it to, and the desire to live to your fullest will not be overlooked. When things become too much to handle, you will feel like you can fit into a normal context, but you can't. Given that the love we develop for life is not something we can direct towards ordinary activities, we only have necessities as our objectives.

Once you dedicate yourself to a certain path, your whole life begins to depend on that idea, although a lot can bring sadness, however, is it really necessary to be depressed all the time? That you never had things easy, that you couldn't socialize like everyone, yet you did find an opportunity to live whatever was meant for you. So if something is not destined for your whole existence, when is the appropriate time to abandon it? Do you let go when you're still in love with it, or just from the beginning you allow it to pass given that it doesn't form part of who you are in the future?

Are we guilty of letting go early, or we should hold on to what we use to be, even if it's not true, but what if we couldn't make a living from it? Regardless of what you do, it can't be life any more, whatever attempts you make will keep worsening situations, and the more you hang around, is just holding your progress back, and denying yourself an opportunity to live for true love early.

Can someone deny you a chance to be happy with everything that you know, or we are the ones that denied ourselves the truth about life? Or our lack of happiness emerges from those situations that you didn't see their worth, that you allowed to pass, and now that they have passed, you realize that they've been worth everything to live for.

Does it feel any good to be going through situations where you know so much could've been well, you see it clearly that you deserve better. Yet because you have dreams so much is left back, and for some reason you keep struggling to have things easy, however, when everything has passed, and you got what you wanted, do you have any regrets? Knowing that we can't make peace with so much that we have allow to pass, the love we feel for each other, we wanted it every day, to live for it, and it has been the pain that we carry which we cannot come to terms with.

We feel like there's abuse to the situation, that we couldn't be what we wanted easily, or share the love we have for one another, and that we had been held from being together. Things must be easy, we want to live without having to sacrifice anything or being denied what we care for the most.

True love is created and meant for us to embrace it, and there's no situation that we can't stand if we have love, but can you face the universe without it? Is what gives us the energy to thrive through any adversary. What uplifts you, or really need to cope with the life that you living? I find that a worthwhile partner is very necessary for our everyday happiness. If you could find one, maybe you can forgive the world, for your motives would've led you to what you desired most.

To have a good relationship means a lot to us people who want to achieve something motivated by creativity. Love becomes one of the most important treasures that we've acquired, it resembles that inner person who lives beneath the surface of our soul. Reflects what you carrying inside, what we want can be driven by anything, but that is brought forth by goodwill. For all that you have given, the same must be returned back to you multiplied.

Chapter Fourteen

Gift of Life

Things had just begun to make sense, when you learned that to be without the one that you love, is like having a huge mountain to climb ahead of you. For all your life you will feel denied an opportunity to live, and be happy with yourself. You will constantly be fighting situations and dealing with problems that came through that path of relationships.

You might fail to understand a lot of things from lacking someone to share issues of paramount importance with. As there is no easy way to confront what you doing except that you have to use your brain, and you won't be able to know everything with your head.

We are not meant to fight all the battles with our minds, or let alone win whatever difficulty we face with our thoughts. We constantly need love to guide us on how to approach things well, and then you realize that life shouldn't be a struggle. Without that tenderness of who we are everything just comes back to depress you, as we are not built to know so much, there's only enough that we can figure out with our understanding.

To succeed you have to know more than is required of one, as everything is standing in your path, and you can try with your whole heart to master your way around things, only to find that a little challenges your entire being. Now you have to establish a plan that can help you pass through so much, which might try to hold you back from achieving a lot that you desire.

There won't be anything you don't understand, if you are to survive all that there is around you, there will be a lot of battles that you go through just to have a normal life. So to find peace at the end of the day, you must be able to surrender yourself to someone who deserves who you are.

As you stare at the world, you're somehow surprised that there could be that one individual, who not only are you indebted to, but you owe them your entire existence. They are here to rescue you from all the frustrations that one can go through in a lifetime. You must love them so much, even if they are not with you every day, you always know your heart is safe with that person.

You allow someone to walk away from you just a little bit, and not that they don't matter, you only allowing them to live. You refuse to be true to a person because you own them, you don't want to limit their horizon. People are not only important when you control or possess them, they must be free to be human beings for all that they are, and be able to do what they like or know anything there is to understand about life.

The same could be applied with regard to everyone we care about, parenting as well must love you enough to want to see the good in the human being that you are. Never hold your children back, and you mustn't abuse them or try to own them in any way, especially when it's not necessary.

Your love given unconditionally means a lot to the ones you have in your cycle of care, as part of the things you cannot change about the person that you are. If you are not meant to take life away from human beings, you just can't. Give everything you are to those who need you the most, so that you can feel alive, and do not ever complain about the role you play in their lives. You hold on to knowing that this human or individual is worth so much to me, and they will always mean that.

That is regardless of what you have done to allow life to live through that person, even if it has allowed them to be successful, you don't hold them back on anything. Not only when it comes to life in general, but all of it, you make peace with knowing that you did the best that you could, to give them a gift that will open doors to eternity, and you have blessed them as well.

To care must come easy, or allowed to be a natural tender that you have towards others, even when you've done something unique. Especially one of those things which maybe you created that has given life to so many and made you stand out above the rest. You constantly remember the ought you made with yourself and the objective you have towards other people who will benefit from that idea.

That whatever the impact your understanding has had on those human beings, it doesn't give you the right to think you know what's best for them, or to just want more out of their lives, you let them live freely. On the other hand don't be blindfolded by the time you've spent with people, to make you think less of them. They still deserve who they are, and they're free to be whatever they need to be, and they can choose who they want to become.

When you see what you've done, be able to take pride in yourself, more than you did before knowing that you did well as you are not that kind of a person, who could try to hold people back. Even when life doesn't allow you to be happy from the difficulties we encounter as we go through creation. Be glad as you know that somehow the world does find a way to repay us for what we do, you could come across someone, whom might become everything to celebrate about living the way you do. From there on so much might become an inspiration that you feel courageous to be forever motivated about doing great things all the time.

Is rare to find someone who cares about you, we live in a world filled with chaos, where people could want so much out of you, which could alter your entire purpose. Deep down inside you know I'm not a bad person, but there are times where human beings could expect you to give something that you don't have, and that makes you feel like there's a need to compromise the objectives you have for life.

People have expectations, they live to see what they like, mostly we are not what so many make us to be, and deep inside is sad, when someone want to turn you into something that you not. The worse part about it, is that you could be living through your own ideas, and that gives no one the right to interfere in your life. Regardless of the perception you have of the world there's no need to be deprived of certain rights as you're not what so many expected of you.

At times there's nothing that we can do to please human beings, especially with the only chance we have to be human, and that is regardless of what a person could've done for you. For some reason that can hold you back, when you are unable to give them what they want, and that's not good, being a kind individual is allowing people to make their own decisions.

When you have done everything to resemble that you care, you just want to be free to have whatever you desire. You can give life to human beings, but yours as well matters and must be cared for. Sometimes we can do things that shows understanding for what we doing, is when you've created life in a way that changes so much about what we've known. Yet even that cannot satisfy you if you have no one to love you.

For someone to be completely satisfied with what they're doing at the end of the day, there must be someone you come back to, and maybe that could work very well. For in love we get to share this beauty that we see in each other, that answers and opens every door. Is when you standing in front of a person and your heart has no questions about why you are that kind of an individual, and regardless of what you know, or seek out of life that is able to give you complete joy.

At times we have the need to work as we feel very talented and that we can add an impact, or do a lot of good. However, if on the other hand you have no one to love you, is very saddening like there's no need to keep doing what you devoted to, given that everything is against what you are. You might find yourself stuck, and without a clue on how to handle such a challenge, and with no idea on what to do, as it could be the only thing you know how to be.

You want to do the right thing, yet situations are somehow too difficult to cope with, is not that you not sure of what you doing. It could be that human beings want to change the results of what you engage in, how you think, and act towards your goals and motivation. We are never given an easy task, sometimes we found ourselves bind against what we desire, so that people can influence the outcome of what we do.

Should we make it happen by force, the gift, against life, beauty, and love, as everything can become too precious to have at once. So if anything was to stand in your way, what would you do to bring whatever you want into reality? As part of the people that we are, can have this huge discrimination amongst each other. Even when you think you're doing the best to help in a situation, you realize that you only betraying your soul.

You can look and compare all there is out there, to what you doing, only to find that you've done everything required of someone, yet it can never be enough, only because of the hatred that can exist between us as people. The talent can be stolen from someone, the gift of love, life, education, and whatever you can produce as part of your understanding. Knowing very well that things cannot be made to happen beyond what you've resembled, so how do you handle such pressure? You continue to embrace the knowledge, against every difficulty that you encounter.

"You cannot make a difference as well", do not say something is bad, and if you were given a chance you would do better. When you have that opportunity you learn from those who mistreated human beings, and do the same to others as well, that won't bring any change. You could have known so much, however, do not try and force your ideas into people, regardless of how difficult situations might be, that is the best one can offer to create greatness in the world.

On the other hand loneliness can take over your entire being trying to get things right. I waited for someone every day, and that person was never there, we were living in that old world, distanced from each other as people who want to be intimate with one another. You wish for a specific individual and they never came close. So we wanted to be weak for love to be easy, yet life wouldn't let us be, we had to carry it through, and what you long for never became possible when you required it to.

You have to wait for that opportunity to arise so that you can resemble how you feel deep in your heart, that didn't come so easy as well. So if you do get that chance you have to make use of it to show all that you are, which could prove your commitment. Although some things do exists outside the law of love and discipline, at times there's nothing that others can do to be part of it.

We don't choose this people that we are, and you cannot overlook the need to exercise some rules or just to have good morals. You could've worked hard more than one could ever understand to prove your worth and that you do know what you doing, however, failure to handle pressure can undermine everything that you stand for.

Anyone can be what they want to, there's nothing holding you back, is just that when you have shown them the greatness you hold in your heart, you will see at the end that others wish the same for you as well. For whatever you have done for them, you must find your way and be free, and in this life that you have given yours too.

My desire was into the beauty of creation, and what can you do when you know is not something that we can become easily? And what if you were not prepared for everything, and somehow time can steal so much that you use to be, and now it has turn out to be the only way you can have what you need in this existence.

Time can steal so much that you valued as you try to figure a way to be what you dream of, and more than that, this can spread throughout your entire life. That you can come to lose the direction towards your personal affairs and relationships. At the end you find the world holding you back with what you use to be, aiming at your heart with everything that you want to achieve.

Although at some point if you insist on going forward you can discover so much that a lot can never recognize what it is that is being invented. Things like ideas, lifestyle, love, and more life situations that you know that even though I had been denied the right to live freely or do what I want, yet now that I have come to succeed, then everyone will learn to follow.

From what you've created a new way for people to live their lives will be invented, it always starts with a single person, and if no one ever does, everyone just stays back and never makes a move. However, if someone says I'm going through this path, so many will follow to show appreciation for what you doing, and they will never question anything. Just like that you have given life, unlike destroying the gift before it can be seen and lived.

Follow the path that you have chosen among so much that there is out there, if you want to live in a way that satisfies your heart. Even though you have to do more than you're required to, if you are to survive in the real world, as everything could be competitive. Life is always aimed at by other people as well, there is so much that as human beings we need from creation. Whether your path is difficult or not, you have to keep on going, knowing that whatever can stand in your way can aim high at your goals.

Do you believe in what you doing, can it defends itself against all odds, is it an idea that can surpass human understanding, can you find your way through it, to the real world as you had desired for things to be?

Looking at what you have you must realize where you are, it must be where you belong, but is it something that can protect you from deep within, and can it defend you from everything in spirit? You might have never expected things to go this far, still do not overlook how the world has changed, and how much is required of someone to be accepted, from there you might become something that people really approve of. So do not fail yourself as someone living in your own creativity, the only thing that make sense to you is your efforts and what you thinking.

As you get to experience the universe through your understanding, you might see so much that is not how you imagined the world to be. Still, do not victimize as well, even when you don't understand the kind of challenges you facing, and what it means.

Consider the fact that you mustn't learn from those who have victimized the world and decide to be someone who applies the same method when dealing with other people. So proceed cautiously with goodwill and positive attitude, do what you need done according to how you must, and without fear, Knowing that the love you have in your heart, will guarantee you complete safety and happiness at the end.

I was not right about everything all the time, at some point I had to acknowledge that so much that happened, was because I didn't have knowledge of what I was doing. If one has clarity of what they do then there's no reason for someone to complain, about whether the outside world is right or wrong.

At the end, it could be that if you are wrong you can only harm yourself, and right will defend itself. You don't need to come up with excuses that humanity doesn't understand or maybe they just can't relate to what you doing. Whatever it is can it be correct, can you prove that your knowledge is accurate instead of fighting because that won't give you the results that you want?

As you go on living for your own goals, you can reach at that point where you prove that you understand precisely what you doing, and be able to avoid that mistake which can occur of delaying yourself by engaging in something you not sure about. What are you trying to create, how can you be certain that what you loved so much, will also be liked by everyone that comes into contact with it, will it make sense to people out there?

So much that we engage in can steal our lives away from us, imagine an inventor that discovered an invention at his twenties. Only to study his discovery for nine years and beyond, to be clearly understood by human beings and be able to go public, and then to the rest of the world. The time that he missed, to some people meant a lot, and when you come back you realized that you never lived for the rest of your life.

There's so much that life could have done for you in that period of time, so do you believe in that thing which has discovered your understanding? Because you could come back only to find that you've missed a lot of time, and the results of that never got you that far. It must be an idea that you can argue about, one that you can prove to the world that you know it's right and can stand above all that is out there. Being confident that you are correct and you're able to differentiate it from the next person, resemble that it is necessary, and at some point you let it speak for itself.

Can it stand against the whole world? Given that people do not want to be disturbed by ideas which are not useful to who they are. So if you want their attention you need to be standing at a place where we know that you understand what you saying.

"Right, what kind of right are you talking about, and what does it mean to the entire world, are you right about yourself, both woman and man, or right about your creation? I was after creating what is right about us people, regardless of whether you black, white, Indian or Asian, that is the right that matters, no matter how difficult situations could be, that is something which can be able to defend itself and those who represent it."

Love, life, and happiness are all driven by the same thing, and when that thing drives every one of us, who doesn't deserve to be part of it, or anyone to commit to them? And that being the quality we seek out of this world. To me every person must have a chance to realize what they know or dreamed of, coming to reality, whatever idea you have should be achievable no matter what. No one's thought are not enough, it should be possible regardless of how difficult it could be, living in a universe where a child's dream can become a possibility to greatness.

Chapter Fifteen

Measure of Love

Commitment is the measure of love, and the only reason why we must give in to one another honestly, you don't relax in a relationship, or forget for one minute how to care. Knowing very well that you're doing everything that needs to be done with someone. What is the purpose of being intimate with each other, if you're not completely in it with your whole heart?

You know that from deep within you, is not there, you don't mean it, you just enjoy being together for fun. One shouldn't be wondering about how committed you are to them, however, we are not always honest about what we say to our partners, especially how much the other means to you.

If the devotion we had, could be measured, then people would have known how to love each other truthfully, and it would be easy to see if someone is lying or not. Also considering the fact that within a relationship there would have to be a level that no human being can ever exceed unless their fully committed to loving one another.

If you ever go beyond that point, you have to be completely dedicated to each other honestly, it could be the reason why people cannot always have what they want when it suits them. Relationships go through stages of growth, you have to be heading somewhere if you are to remain together, and you just can't be focused on the pleasures of the bodies forever.

Love is undeniable, it's always good for human beings to be with one another, but that which is shared among each other needs loyalty to give, and to enjoy. As someone can lie about caring for you, knowing that deep in their hearts there's nothing that they feel.

You cannot be involved in the depths of relationships without true devotion, there's a level where it might be unnecessary to continue unless you've given yourself to each other permanently. That's where things starts to be confusing, is when you reach at that place where it's inappropriate to exceed in a human being unless you're both fully in love. Even if you were to stop there, it would have effects on each one of you, because you would have given too much of one another without a well-defined purpose.

How do you give yourself to a person if you are not prepared to be with that human being forever, this is where a lot questions the value we have towards each other. No matter what you might think of the other, something has to exist that looks into the well-being of humanity in terms of relationships and commitment. We cannot deceive ourselves thinking that there could have been anything that mattered more than what we are to one another.

It must be something that we're prepared to share honestly, we need to involve ourselves deeply in it. At first if love could be measured, the best way would be by the devotion we resemble towards one another, how much we made love to each other or cared for the other deeply. If you truly care about your partner so much, why not take it to the next level, is that part which we need to understand, how is given honestly and by what can it be evaluated?

"So it is said that love is deep, or deeper than the ocean, and anything we have ever known, or felt for each other, and if it could be measured from within the sea, the measurement would have been the sort of an island. No matter how big and deep the island can be, within it there's another beginning of the water going far below. Descending deeper than any man or woman can ever go, deep within the depth of the island water continues to form part of the sea.

The ocean represents true love and devotion for one another, and the island is there to represent our lack of seriousness and issues that could stand between us and being truly in love. Beneath the island, in the depth of the sea is how our commitment for each other is measured, the island measures our full dedication. When you haven't given in to the other completely, when the "I" in you still exists, so when you're fully devoted to loving your partner, the "I", disappears, you become the ocean or love."

Is true that life can be mastered, however, this is based on the fact that the one you've devoted yourself to, will always be the only person who has ever mattered more than anyone. It could be about the passion that flows within a dedicated relationship. Love grows with how much we give to our union, the longer we stay together, the deeper we develop the bond for one another, yet we cannot remain there forever. You have to advance to the next level of growth, do not fool yourselves by being ignorant of each other from the activities happening between your lives, you have to be satisfied with your devotion and grow with time.

It is always your responsibility to wait for someone whom you will love deeply, to spend the rest of your life with you, once you find true love you cannot be able to commit to anyone again. What we give to each other becomes permanent, we can never come out of a relationship in the same way in which we were, we lose some part, or the essence of who we are in every turn.

You wonder, trying to understand why was I supposed to love this person forever, why can't it be true love with whoever comes every day? Maybe it could be that there can only be a room for one, there is never enough space for another again, once you accommodate someone, there is no going back.

I wanted things to be easy, be able to welcome another person, and that individual is supposed to feel the same as the one before, find genuine love in my heart and never look back again. At times we can't let go of each other, is just trying to say that if there's anything to admire about a human being, then there will always be that thing to hold on to.

Why can't we deal with separations very well, and the real reason why we had to separate, the truth behind our irreconcilable differences. Being honest in dealing with the issue, and looking at it on a psychological level as well. Understanding what is it that really breaks two people apart, and then their separated from everything that has ever mattered, whatever they had is gone, the only one you truly loved has left your life forever.

True love has a spiritual connection that exists between human beings that have given themselves to each other honestly, is when you surrender your heart to someone when you still matter. Though we come from different worlds as man or woman, yet arriving at that place where we are what the other need the most, and giving them your true self. Whatever comes after that can never be what it used to be, it will be love, however, on a different platform, not where you were the most important to whom you loved before.

There were times where relationships were once real in our lives, but as deep as we are willing to surrender to each other, it does disappear from where it used to be true. The minute you leave someone for another, the heart becomes weak to commit, you can't be able to give from your essence again. As true love cannot always be available, you can't go back to the beginning where love was pure, to your first day, commitment, or marriage.

In relationships you have to be fully alert, and very knowledgeable about giving in to the other, given that when love is no longer true, you can fall prey or be subjected to so much that exists out there. You could become subject to situations, that have been created or mastered by other people, whether you understand or not, when true love has disappeared, a lot can come in between couples.

Sometimes we don't just separate as people, we fail to understand our role in being together, our lack of devotion can be one of the issues that can weaken a relationship. That is when you've failed to play your part in caring for your partner, or maybe that can wait for some time. Our commitment can still be measured by how much we love each other, and if that could be the measurement, who loves more than the other?

To have doubts or questions in a relationship, about the other that completes who you are, or cares for you, can affect a human being's focus to love, and that can ruin so much that true unions stands for. We don't stop to ask or question if anything is still real or not, we carry on loving and living through it. Love waits for no one, it continues to create our lives and the world every day, the doubts in your heart must be the only thing you running away from. As something that can come between two people who are meant for each other and destroy what they have, or steal away that thing which has brought them together.

When you allow hesitations or doubts to exist in your relationship, you open the gates for the spirit that lives to tear down the good in everything to come and dwell in your life. I had liked this part about being human, to have had an opportunity to love and be loved by someone special, then everything automatically accepts you, to care and you're also cared for.

About the measure of commitment, how much do you love each other, or need one another? That's all that the world will constantly ask about your dedication into being in a relationship, however, if it was a Christian marriage you wouldn't want to be questioned with regard to that. You would probably know the value of your partner, as you understand that true love doesn't come easy, and the discipline as well.

Everything we do with each other, measures the dedication we have amongst one another, and that can allow anything to judge our lives. As long as it is based on true love for whatever there is, to survive human development and evolution, you must always remain true to that part of life, in order to evolve with time.

I don't know if I should have wondered about what it takes to find the right partner, somehow I knew that it was something very crucial to be concerned about. To consider everything that brings it all together, and make it happen, to be finally content as you've find the one. We had been born in a concealed world, in terms of making human beings aware of how important some parts of our lives could be. If we understood clearly how imperative things are, then we would have known what to do, and how to take whatever there is into serious consideration.

To avoid making mistakes that will come back to cost us a lot that we value, love is a commitment, you don't just engage in it, and then give up on caring about the person. Relationships comes with responsibilities, to care and nurture for the other party, you just don't go after some things, you value the whole soul and what embodies it.

To be single is one disadvantage towards life, you might suffer lack of understanding and clarity on certain issues, you might be unable to think clearly about what matters the most. There are necessary things that one needs to understand about being a person, yet are the kind that are of major concern when you are involved with someone. Like sharing the truth, goals, and your intimate thoughts, and that being part of taking responsibilities for growth.

If we were to live alone, one would even reach to the masters, trying to understand things that you can easily grasp with your thoughts if you were with someone. Responsibilities that you must take that resembles maturity, issues about life, and love, that are hidden just below the surface of our commitment.

There is something that I struggled to understand, and it was one of the most important parts of our lives, given that if you feel the need to be truly loved. There must be responsibilities that you have undertaken, there has to be something that you trying to achieve, if you ever are to find happiness at the end.

What comes first, Is it love, or responsibilities for the future? Being able to understand what matters the most, and going after that thing so that you can achieve your overall goals. When is it enough to know that you have done the best that you could to accommodate someone, and be able to arrive at that place called true love?

Regardless of how guilty one could've been, being accepted by the other that you're past experiences or encounters no longer matters. Now you can start over and work your way through a loving heart, walking pass that old self into a brighter tomorrow. Passing through those errors which could've occurred that made it difficult to understand how did you separate with the only one who was meant for you?

We cannot be meant not to ever find love again, something must exists out there that will care for us once more, and it must be enough to give someone a second chance, unless if there's some entity which is pleased with our loneliness.

Then it would explain this external force that keeps interfering with our happiness, how our past keeps coming back to haunt us as if our love life are controlled by something outside our lives. So if relationships can be influenced by the things we did forever, then a lot about us could be against what we need in the future.

We come from situations where we went through heartbreaks, that have left us torn apart, and one can really use a break from the kind of loss that we have endured. As we are all student to this subject of love, we are never sure of what we doing, and so many of us could've failed to easily understand how to care or resemble true love. To commit yourself beyond those premature stages that could measure someone's commitment between two people loving one another.

Beside our lack of devotion, maybe an outside force has interfered with our lives, other than just our past failures. Yet it would take more than hatred to interrupt the flow of love between two people loving each other honestly. Could we have failed to master our destiny and now we have become the subject to so much happening around us? And all that has opened the doors for confusion to rule our lives. Now at the end it feels so unfair for one's life to be controlled by situations which have come to pass, that is without having to point fingers to where could the problem be emerging from.

It resulted in the majority of human beings not to have succeeded in finding a worthwhile relationship and settled for anything irrelevant to true love. I had studied my whole life and acquired knowledge on paramount subject about reality, yet I have never been fortunate, to find true love or happiness. Makes me wonder what really steals away that tender which we all seek to break out of this imprisonment, that being without a good partner can push you to.

Can there be something that has truly stolen something of that much value to us? Maybe it could have occurred that someone got ahead of themselves and tried to take advantage of what they know about our lives. Still, even with all the knowledge and power of understanding I couldn't think of anything like that, I just couldn't let myself be controlled by that kind of hatred.

Yes we could've been wrong for overlooking what we had, and that could've allowed for so much to disturb our focus. Maybe things are not meant to be like that, yet it serves someone very well not to understand why people should be thinking love, engaging in it, and loving each other truthfully. That is what motivates this thing that keeps interfering in our lives seeking to separate human beings as we could've lost our purpose to care, and we can no longer commit from deep within our soul.

It's an act that exists in some individuals, only that it could be influenced by our way of doing things, our sloppiness with regard to enduring the pain of relationships. The way we lack courage and commitment could be the main reason for our failure. Given that love on its own is very strong and can withstand everything that there is, only if you give it the energy by serving it honestly.

Maybe relationships becomes difficult for those who are eager to master situations. Everything that you want becomes depended towards the path you have chosen, and somehow even what we are from deep within which is meant to combine us with the ones we love the most, stops doing its function. Our inner goals, the quest we have to be more slowly separates us from those we long to be with, without realizing how it has happened you just stop loving the way you need to. You keep wondering how that has interfered with finding the right person, as it feels like someone can make a room, if only they had a heart that truly cares.

Could it be about loving the right person, as it might happen that you will arrive at that place, yet it might not happen when someone hoped it would, therefore it needs one to have committed themselves selflessly. If not, there could later be a problem given that whatever you thought existed or what attached one to the other could never work like you hope it would. Then having to deal with the separation thereof might have that much effect on both of you as you have failed to be strong for love.

Yes love was once innocent, as much as we need it, and it was all free, however, with the way of our lives, priorities and everything, so much has become complicated. Our needs are never at that point of simplicity, a lot that we want has value attached to it. So our ambitions have turn out to be the solution, whatever goal you have, has a specific reward that will come to exist at the end, and if you succeed that objective is able to produce your heart's desires.

Although some things could occur from within the relationship and ruin everything that we value. However, to lack growth and commitment for one another can jeopardize all that we live for. It could happen that we might have been in love for some time, yet not willing to advance through the stages of life, and now everyday has become a struggle.

As we keep going, time becomes a defying factor, is when you arrive at that place where you have been doing something for a very long period. Yet you lack that true motivation to give in completely to each other. We need to grow every day, getting more involved in love, sharing so much that we have, and the relationship becoming transparent, and like that things are just easy to live through.

Within a worthwhile relationship people are not supposed to be separated by anything, whether one could have failed their objectives we are in it together. They could have not understood things clearly, but they have each other. Is it not true that love is meant to be our ultimate objectives? We can take chances in so much that exists, yet there, is where we need to be sure. It doesn't matter what we don't know how to be, as long as we know how to do everything for us, and what we have, and in a way that satisfies both parties.

Everybody wants to be something great in life, only that it doesn't have to affect our relationships, in the essence of love, we don't need to attach anything to it. Although things have changed more than ever, and everything that we want now comes at a price, we can still try to look at each other beyond the effects of modernization.

With exposure to this modern way of living, people have developed a lot of needs, and if you cannot satisfy them all. It might have an impact on the way you wanted to spend every day of your life with someone that you care about. Not because we don't have true love anymore, so much is just there to ruin what we had. The simplest tender we have ever needed, now come at a price, and if you don't fulfill that, you feel like the whole world has been turned against you.

Although issues are always there and trying to come between those who seek to be a good couple. We are at times discriminated against the fact that we cannot afford to have a worthwhile relationship where both partners are satisfied with their lives. With all the increasing needs you can get lost thinking that love doesn't exist, and it does, and it can be found where is true when you have worked hard to have all that is necessary.

You can try to be someone who resembles love, care, and sincerity, only that life comes with responsibilities. You need to have accomplished so much on your own, to show that you're prepared for a relationship in every situation. However, if you there with the aim to commit you can succeed even when it cost so much to make your partner happy. The willingness you have in your heart will lead you through until you reach at that place where you live in a healthy loving environment.

Things had never been good enough for us to be free as well, we live in a world of one man against another, and if the other wins, also manipulates everything to work in his favor. For the loser there won't be a resting place, you can't find anything to do or anyone to love for that matter. As long as you trying to engage in whatever could make you happy, life will feel like a struggle, a lot will leave you with emotional stress.

Coming from that world, now you understand why you have to work hard, to arrive at a certain area where you get your fair share of life. Honestly knowing that if you cannot afford to live in a good and comfortable environment then you cannot exercise your right to be loved by the one you deserve to be with. Failing to master our destiny is worse than being cursed, and for a very long time, you can look for someone to be with, of which you can never know where to find.

Though if you look at it carefully, it feels like a situation that had been worked out by man and woman, who live with the eager to deceive humanity of the reality that we've known. That you are a normal human being, and you have been given as much as you desire, that whatever you seek out of life, exist in you as well, and it has always been your birth right.

No one doesn't deserve anything from life, no matter what you are or seek to understand, something must exist for you out there. Even if it's just a long-standing relationship that has worked you to a lonely situation, it is not the end of the world. You can still find yourself within the context of love, you can come out of every setback the way you were, you don't need to change a thing about yourself, as we are all born deserving.

Love is something that has always been real in any human being, no one has the right to steal away that tender from you. Go on knowing that happiness is the only gift that we've inherited from this divine creation, and everyone does deserves that chance to be happy.

We were once incompetent with it comes to loving each other, we couldn't be fully devoted like we're supposed to. We had been caught living in false illusion, we were stuck in a world obsessed with challenging everything that we are. Yet it isn't much that we required from this life, it is just the basics to being human in general. The right to be loved, the need to a loving family, in a civilized society that felt like you asking for too much.

Chapter Sixteen

Masters of Life

What sees into everything that we doing, whether good or bad, our hidden intentions, or motivation towards any act? Who brings justice to so much that we are, or knows whatever it is that we do, and keeps the record of all our deeds? We would be locked in cages, where we couldn't make it out even if we wanted to, people would just get away with anything.

In the past someone could have done some pretty harmful things, at the end they just want to escape the law. Yet in the world that we live in there's something that is always watching over us, to ensure that everyone gets their fair share of life. However, some are still found wandering about what is it that looks into our entire activities.

People would be left to themselves to wonder all their lives, if there was nothing that looks into the well-being of humanity. No matter what man can invent, there will always be something that has seen everything, which is watching over us human beings, and that can be able to free us from whatever can try to interfere with our progress.

We would be completely overpowered by situations, laws would be burnt only to suit the needs of specific individuals. Not even any one of us would have the courage to do anything with regard to that, or just to be taken into consideration.

Life would be a complete takeover, depriving human beings of their right to be normal, everything would be taken away from everyone that had no idea of what's going on, or just to have any clue of what is happening in the world. We would keep on living with no direction of where we going, even if you know what to do, or had any ambitions towards creation, what would you do about it? As your rights wouldn't matter.

That's how limited life would be for so many against everything that there is, to limit human essential needs, withholding their rights to be free. It would become one of the most difficult situations to cope with, for those who understand what is happening, as a lot of important things would have been taken away from them.

People would be surviving with faith, but without any power or motivation towards life, a lot would turn out to be very hard for human beings just to get through the day. When you have your lives subjected to the toughest situations of this world, it would need one to prepare themselves for all that there is, if you are to survive.

The masters of life governs the relationship we man and woman have with each other, as well as creation. Our thoughts and feelings about anything don't apply, it allows for things to be what they must be, even if is against so much that there is in our lives. With all that there is available, people can try to manipulate situations to overlook the basic rights to being a normal person. People deserve to be happy, they want to understand that they are being considered from deep within.

A lot can try to change our path to being normal people, and device things which anyone can understand that this isn't the way we have chosen for ourselves, but it is created for human beings to lose their purpose.

You could be someone standing at a certain place, knowing that all you know how to do is to be a good person. Who wants love and believe in it in such a way that you have never known anything except loving a human being. Somehow you are just following the rule of creation, of honoring the beauty that we possess. You understand clearly what is required of you, and you are completely dedicated to achieving that.

You walk the path of creation with faith, and love as your ultimate guide, if you let go of it, you lose a lot that you value, and yourself where you loved. Yet you didn't, you made sure you held on to it, as you believe in it so much and with all that you have. Given that your life's work only accounts or make sense as a good person, in this platform of creativity.

You loved yourself and treasured everything that you know, and worked very hard to achieve great understanding. You never wanted the world to have deceived you, but preferred things the way they are in general. Who could have guessed that at a very early age you would have done something amazing with your knowledge? Yet if you had allowed that opportunity to have passed you, what would you be today?

So much would continuously question you as you move on, that how far gone are you, and does everything make sense? Do you understand your purpose as you go through life, are you still capable of finding the value in things, and how important they are, just like you did before you came of age?

However, it was not with everything that you could've completed on time, you got left back on some other important parts of our daily lives. As you were still discovering the universe, it was through the faith you had to resemble, that you became lost in love and whatever exists outside that path of your focus. The world is never what we expect, our clear purpose to life and relationships can lose its significance, and you become confused from how so much isn't how we hoped it would be.

Pushed by the difficulties of situations we encounter along the way, for some time we could have been made to forget about love, only that we didn't stop loving. We hanged in there with faith, and we saw everything coming to pass, and then we realized that to be faithful is to believe in the ideas that have founded our perception. To have traveled a journey for the first time, not caring or knowing what the future holds, and yet you never stopped or changed the objectives of your purpose, which can alter the outcome of your entire understanding.

We wanted to focus on creativity, being free to do whatever our minds desired, and without having to wonder about achieving those goals. Living every moment with no regrets of what we have become, what could steal away that tenderness we have towards life? However, we live in a world where you know that it is wrong for us to be part of anything, and you can try to correct certain things, only that there's just too much that needs to be fixed.

A world so completely wrong, that it has been made to be suitable for certain people, but not everyone, you fight for self-worthiness, trying with everything you have to find satisfaction, yet there's none. Stuck in a place where you want recognition, and you can't blame anyone is you who has chosen your own path, which never led you to love, now you want your way back to someone's arms.

By now you have been upset from reality for a very long time, and as much as you want to come back from wherever you from, if you haven't discovered something unique you will be wasting your energy. Regardless of the eagerness you have to be part of everything, somehow life has moved forward, and you have missed a lot, and you can't have your old self back, even the love you knew has disappeared.

Whether you have goals or not, there's so much you cannot understand about love. If you haven't committed all that you are to someone early, you just become confused. You find yourself left with nothing to live for, yet a good relationship could herd you, and you become content in those situations that life had become meaningless. You begin to remember who you are, and look away from so much that keeps fighting with you, where you are a human being, as you have lost your purpose.

You can begin something not knowing where is headed, only that to you, it means a lot given that achieving it will change your life entirely. It doesn't matter whether is a good or a better plan, without determination it means nothing, you have to give in to it completely, and regardless of what happens along the way, there's no going back.

You have to find a way to succeed through that path which you have chosen for yourself, and without having to sacrifice anything that you are. Even if is just a minor idea that you have, don't give up on how you wanted the outcome to be, use it to harness life. Nurture it until it becomes fruitful, as human beings require more than just a sacrifice, they need healing back to reality.

Though there's so much that can come between your ambitions, and the love you have for someone, as there are others who could have mastered life as well. How they've applied their knowledge in their path to understanding could be different from how you've known things, and that could be difficult to pass through with ease, and be able to realize your goals.

If you really want to master your understanding, sometimes you might be required to go against everyone that you care about, as they cannot clearly understand what you want to see realized. For a very long time you could need to keep traveling, and forget about whatever could be going on outside the path you have chosen.

Although along the way you might constantly ask yourself if you still care or not? Only that you mustn't forget what made you choose this person that you are as the best solution available to be a normal human being. We wanted a lot achieved, and as much as we needed cannot be found easily, so this has become our one way to have.

There are a lot of stages where things occur, and in all these levels there's something to value, but when you have that only way to live through, you look away from everything happening outside your path, so that you can have your ambitions realized. So many can admire your work, and so much can be done against the human being that you are, however, yours is that goal you seek to bring forth. Sometimes we just go into it, this life knowing that whatever we doing makes sense to us, and it will be like that for the rest of your journey, until you achieve your desires.

You mustn't allow situations to dictate you, and give up on your dreams, it is always up to you to be more than just prepared, and even if it means that you died doing the same thing. Whether it feels right or wrong, you give a silent battle that only requires you to gear up in understanding, now that at the end, you have found this world very strong and challenging.

There are a lot of things which might not be how you expected the world to be, yet it mustn't change the way you wanted to achieve your objectives. You could have begun this life from a very early age, and now that you've grown up, it has become something that has founded your perception. Though the path could've been unclear at times, however, if you can only give your whole life to it, you may be surprised that it could turn out to be a great invention which a lot of people, young and old might want so much from it.

When you have clearly defined objectives, no one can refuse to be part of your idea, you must develop your concepts until they become concrete, and easy for everyone to understand. You mustn't be surprised when people want more out of you, is not something that so many engages in every day, so be prepared to excel, by working hard until you see how everything fits in human being's lives.

You mustn't be ashamed to start your foundation that has good morals, dignity, and respect, that is the part you will always be proud of yourself, to have had an opportunity to make a great impact. You could have not known how big and successful it might be or what to benefit from it, however, it could be a chance given with sound understanding to start afresh.

You make sure that you do not benefit from doing anything outside your knowledge which could stand in your way, you grow up straight in that path of your goals even if it isn't easy. Only that if you can ever understand, you could be recognized for it, you might be young, yet you are capable of clarity when you think. Realize the meaning of building your own family that is based in working for greater good.

It might not be easy, only that it will mean everything, you could have not thought about it at first, when you were still at the beginning, that one day you will build a legacy of love and great understanding. You also appreciate the transformation because when you began approaching this life, you couldn't change anything, however, true love took over everything and steer your fate to success.

There's something in spirit that is very depended in honesty, and it judges our lives based on our decisions to have been good or bad. When you have fought for a very long time to understand, you find that you must have won with love, it must always be what guarantees your happiness.

It matters not what the other is doing, what's important is that you carry your objectives with honesty, and when your goals were not clearly defined with love as the ultimate outcome. You know that it suffocated you and that you couldn't find a place where you belong, and in that case you lingered anywhere you could find a space to rest. Clearly by now you understand that your life has become dependent on your kind decisions to be progressive in all areas.

It's good to have realized your goals and achieve whatever you were looking for, to possess the kind of knowledge that brought you closer to understanding, and when everything is completely clear maybe you can have peace. That is the life for those who have dedicated themselves in doing greater things until they realize their goals being achieved honestly.

However, for those who never cared about that path, the way for them is different, how quick it might be to witness your thoughts becoming a reality. You just make one unworthy decision and the next morning you will find that all you have ever wanted has come to be, only that peace, and true love might not be easy to reach for.

The truth on the other hand has no turning point, you must keep going in the direction of love, hoping that when you reach the end, true love will transform everything into success. Now we can be able to say that it is the levels that we have passed that became the measure of our faith. Is when you become faithful to a certain idea more than anyone can ever keep up or be able to hold you back. Then you know you can never be weighed down, part of who you are will forever be working for that concept and the greatness of this world.

The strength you will find from the outcome of your work is amazing, after passing so many stages of existence, you will arrive where your ideas create your own platform. Only that you mustn't forget the one rule that has founded humanity which everyone adheres to, that a way of life is meant to be followed, and you will have so many following you as well.

Finding your own path will always be your greatest strength, unlike following everyone where they go, you could come across so many setbacks. People's thoughts are different from what we've always expected, there could be so much you won't understand, and the issue of who mastered that part of our lives, and how they've achieved it. Who returned with life from where we had died, or brought us back from where we couldn't see what we doing, as it is where we all got lost.

Breaking through your understanding or mastering your way of life could refer to anything that introduces a good idea, or a business, which will come and change people's ways, believes, and lifestyles, and it will remain part of human being's lives forever.

It must be able to open that door where we had been locked in change, or stuck in complete darkness, which could have been the reason of being overpowered by something bad or an outside influence. By then when everything has been taken away from people, they couldn't even find anything worth celebrating about being human. Arriving at that level of understanding must motivate life to be worthy and very exciting.

Sometimes you will see, at times the vision might be obscure, as you travel on your own you will get to understand so much, beside the fact that you may find yourself living alone and broken-hearten. Things could have been clear and made good sense when you were growing up, yet if you can ever fall prey to a different way of doing things. You will begin to realize that your world has never collapsed like it did, you will acknowledge that now you have met the encounter of your life.

Though you need to understand that you mustn't hate, but standing on the other side of being capable, you must be involved in caring so much. To love is to be alive, it heals some part in us to be always giving ourselves truly, without it there is no peace that you can find, and the rules that you must follow through, could be the most difficult to adhere to. You get to see that it is a way not meant for everyone, we are born and made different by situations, and yours could be to care.

In the short run, it doesn't feel like is how we're meant to live our lives, however, we are young once, and that age passes. All that which you could have done that resembles lack of care disappears, and it matters more than anything to be involved in being part of something reliable, and to be sure that everything you have is meant for you to treasure forever.

You need to ask yourself sometimes or maybe most of the time, what kind of a reality have you experienced? A world obsessed about being bad, or a universe courageous to be good. Here at the center you can be seen weak for the kindness you possess in your heart, though you could be doing more than so many out there, you can still be abused for the purpose you have to love.

You can be denied what you value the most, and pushed by situations until you find yourself living alone, and that can make you develop a negative attitude when you look at the opposite gender. Meanwhile is you who hasn't clearly understood what is required of you. Love is worth holding on to, only that it can disappoint you at times, when you haven't fulfilled your objectives, or when you have failed to define your purpose very well, you could suffer a lot of rejections.

You might feel the kind of hatred no one has ever seen, or which might be hard to understand, what we can learn about each other when so much isn't going well is amazing, it becomes our greatest introduction to this universe. Just that to have learned to love is one beautiful thing, only that, you could've never expected the world to have given such a response, you could see life that you didn't know existed.

However, you mustn't stop, continue to love until you fade away, or reach where it feels like you've stopped caring and loving. You can never know what kind of a feeling is that, yet you still possess the same true love that has founded your principles. When you have promised to do something, keep doing it regardless of everything holding you back, because that's the part in which you have made a promise to this world.

To love and care mustn't be turned into a weakness which one has developed, when people abuse you emotionally as you possess such kindness of the heart. After some time you become strong and stop caring and loving, for what they are doing, yet deep within you that true love for everything will always rule.

We can misunderstand things when it comes to relationships sometimes, yet to serve it, is on its own an entity that needs no introduction. It works every day, and it doesn't stop as long as you have given yourself to it, only that, once you separate yourself from it. You will feel like you have been interrupted by something that knows how to steal away life where it matters.

Now when you are at your complete understanding, you get to understand that life in general has been tough for this age. You must seek for something that you are, and the person you're meant to love, who will be part of everything you want to accomplish. Regardless of how difficult things might be, you need to be sure that you content of that area of yourself, against everything that exists. Even when you look at our faces, you realize that we have been created differently by the situations we encounter.

You must be alert at all times, have well-defined objectives, as the world has advanced and our needs vary, and are very demanding. You need to keep up with things, and as you seek for your way, you must be very quick and get things right as soon as possible. There is some time you can always take for yourself, however, when it comes to work, you must be fully committed, not every day is free.

Most of the time you must do what needs to be done fully, and then you can be able to accommodate something else. There is never time outside this world that you can make it your own, you have to be completely dedicated to working, and focus on it with all that you have.

There are various strategies in which you can live your life, however, to work with love, is a different story altogether, you don't have to take this path, unless you're permanently prepared for it. As you go through situations so much that you put behind are things that you don't have to go back to, with every stage that you pass, transformation takes over your entire being, and you become something new.

As you learn to accommodate the world with love, the way becomes clear, even if so much could've been difficult, as you head to the end you can now have whatever you choose. When you standing at the finishing line and you have mastered your understanding, we hope that everything could be worth your desires. However, you must avoid that evil doing or way of life, don't be found abusing human beings with what you've learned.

Even if the way is difficult, remember that there's something that can come out of any situation, even if it feels bad. As you work with talent so much changes, given that your mind is not as weak as you think it is, the gift can turn anything into a magnificent creation. By continuously working to develop your life with that much enthusiasm, everything will fall in love with you as well.

So much can be said about loving a human being, and it is on its own a tough thing to achieve when you've become an educated person. We could have enjoyed life, yet at the end, the journey of education leads to some place in the world, and love doesn't respond the way it used to, maybe things have changed in value.

We wanted everything to fall into its place, regardless of how one thinks or tries, you realize there can never be a chance to go back to where we had love so easy. The discipline that is brought into the world of education, sophisticates things even more. It is something that we were not prepared to encounter, it becomes difficult to adjust to it, whether physically or spiritually.

One man can make a huge difference, and he is always enough for the world to see what he meant to show them, but just because you have shown them all that you are, it doesn't make you a vulnerable person.

People go through different obstacles, to resemble what they stand for, and you can put so much in line just to have a certain goal realized. At the end when you have shown them all that you are, they don't have to have a hold on you, as you have given them everything that you know. You must be allowed an opportunity to live as well, even if your life is unusual compared to the rest.

There's a proper way in which one can do things. You can make a mistake and people pretend like they didn't see, just don't make a fool of them behind their backs. Well human beings know how to compensate someone's life in full, don't do something unnecessary unless you're sure that you didn't understand completely.

People have the right to love each other, and no one must ever take that away from them, regardless of how you think of yourself. Human beings must be allowed to be whatever they need to be, even if there's something that you know which can steal that tender they have for life, do not take any advantage of that kind of a situation.

Chapter Seventeen

A Way of Life

Love has the power to restore dignity in human lives, if you ever find a meaningful relationship, your heart begins to be at peace. You realize that you have find the true meaning to what you wanted to live for, and without it you have been missing a very important pillar of happiness inside, something very vital to your well-being.

When you are without a good partner, you lose that sense of belonging, and is everyone who goes through this kind of a situation. Who gets treated like they don't belong, as if you don't matter as you've lost your significant purpose?

You have loved before and everything was fine, and after you lost someone that you cared for, then emptiness took over your entire being. As you are without something that defines your inner person, who you are, and what you stand for. It was in that moment and period of your life, when you realized that so much has been taken away from you.

It is not your first time in this journey, you've done it before, when you have been committed to someone in the past, and the world becomes a struggle to understand in terms of finding a perfect partner again. Is not the other who refuses to give in, is you who has lost your purpose to love, more like you are cursed as there's a human being who hates you out there.

A crying heart that blames you for ruining its happiness, for disappointing it, or eventually letting it down. Shouting out to everyone and saying that, "disappoint that person in whatever he desires, he had true love and everything to live for in me".

After a very long time of going through this kind of a situation, you become depressed, from knowing how people will respond to you, and how that will make you feel. Love is strong in leading us towards a greater path or boosting our confidence when dealing with people. It increases your self-esteem, ensuring respect and dignity within your peers, and the pleasure that human beings find in sharing time with you.

The trustworthiness that you resemble, with friends and family, so many are able to trust you easily, and with so much that they have. You become reliable in a way that everyone finds it comfortable around you, and that's how we benefit from these good relationships that we have with each other, however, when is not there you just disappear in shame.

You can always tell when one has loved before, when they have given the true essence of who they are, or losing the most essential part of their lives to someone. You become a subject to reality, whether you left a person, or the other has deserted you, when you've rejected a human being, or maybe is the other who has abandoned your life, you become exposed to that kind of behaviour.

Still, Regardless of how old one can be, if you haven't committed yourself to anyone before, or rejected a person, or someone rejecting you, then you are always welcome in everyone's life. Love is the true essence of who we are, what happens within our relationships, will always influence the reality of what we go through, and that is what affects our lives in physical form, it is the reflection of what we have become.

When you have experienced the depth of a relationship, made love to a deeper level, or shared something special with someone, when you are from within the deepest regions of a commitment, you can easily be felt. You don't live out here, or belong in the same world with other people, you dwell within that realm of reality. As the other leaves you permanently, you are now living without yourself, you begin to live on the outer surface of life, where you are no longer part of.

No one is strong enough to live without love, or let alone surviving the external dimension with nobody to care for them. Maybe if you only tried once or twice, and you haven't been committed, or you not yet born within those deeper levels of a loving communion. When you are from the inner surface of a union between two hearts that were truly beating for each other, you cannot just neglect yourself, you became formed by that oneness.

Relationships are our pillar of strength, you have seen all that being with no one to care for, can do to a human being. You might feel like maybe you will heal, only that you can't, you will go through every season of solitude, and see everything coming to pass. There's a special effect that we develop from being in love, and when you believe in it more than anything, it becomes your way of life.

You can lose so much, and only to remain with your heart when is a loving one, going through every difficulty to the bitter end, until you reach that point of transformation. Surviving all that you encounter, and coming back through love as your only way of life, restoring your dignity, and healing your wounds for the world to make sense again. After breaking up, fighting, or separating with your partner, there's nothing left, from there on so much is meant to destroy the person that you are.

You can't come back, you will only be watching others and wondering about what you use to be, you could even see plenty of people treating you bad, thinking that you've wronged them, but you haven't. If you have lived your life valuing love with all your heart, until it becomes the center of everything that you doing, you cannot just look away from it. That essential quality of who we are is not only meant for our relationships, once it becomes the rhythm of our soul, we become dependent on it, as our point of contact with the world.

True love becomes the deepest of ourselves that we've ever shared with someone, and when that dies, something that lights up our lives from deep within disappears. If you are not strong enough, you cannot keep up, as it is not meant for the weak-hearted, is for those who are prepared to see things come to pass, through the mists and the storms. Then at the end, you are born again, like a normal person who deserves, yet if you haven't gone through this transformation, you won't remember that you once belonged.

This world will never love you like you had been loved before, care for you in the same way you had been cared for by that special person. It will take everything that you are to have a worthwhile relationship once more. You might not reach for it overnight, however, along the way you will remember that you were born deserving, and meant to spend your life with someone worthy of you, and that human being will find the path back to your loving arms again.

Let circumstances not scare you away from finding true love once more, we all deserve greatness in the world, yet at times you can get caught up in situations that are all wrong. Some relationships are not even worth the trouble, is just that making love can give more of who we are, and the after effects of that is being deeply exposed to a lot of vulnerability.

Even if it could be with someone who didn't matter that much, or maybe there was no true devotion. Still, from that kind of intimacy and the exposure to the reality of love, you hurt yourselves, and you both heartbroken. Given that it doesn't matter whether is a commitment or not, the giving of who we are has its measures, and that can draw a person in. Sharing intimacy transforms human beings somewhere so deep, as you don't know what you exchanging with one another.

Relationships can play tricks on human beings, and you cannot believe that if you want to make it happen by force, it will only come back to hurt you more. You cannot always understand everything at once, loving someone requires one to walk the mile of life with understanding. There are times that you might happen not to be where you can attract love, and if you want to keep pushing things, a lot will disappoint you, as you can go through some difficult experience unexpectedly.

When you realize that things don't respond in a positive way, you could need to take some time and understand what is happening within you. Where could you be lacking clarity? It doesn't just happen for people to refuse you, there has to be something wrong.

Concerning love, some don't respond well to a way of life, while others feel good to follow through it, they just want things how they are. For them it feels great to move along with everything, so the minute your mind is not responsive towards the current lifestyle, your world begins to fall into pieces, and that could lead someone to depression.

These are some of the things that can stand between you and the happiness you seeking for. That kind of separation from the one you loved the most can drive you out of the way, deep into a world where you live to question yourself about what happened with the person you use to be. Where could you have made a mistake, or committed an error you didn't understand the repercussions of.

Remember that what we lose in love cannot be repaired overnight, and you can try to justify all that you going through in your current situation. Yet everything is the result of lacking love, to be without that tender of life causes a lot of disturbances in a human being. Whatever you trying to understand from there onward, you just trying to come back to loving a person.

So when you have taken a different journey, the battle is within your heart, you have nowhere else where you are challenged by situations, except that is on the inside. Then at times when you are looking for love, you could come against a lot of difficulty from the difference that you possess. Is when your mind raises questions about what is it that is happening outside, and you don't feel the need to be part of that idea which is creating our lives.

So much will reflect that the life you living doesn't deserve your attention, and if you don't believe for a very long time you will be fighting the same battle to come back to reality. However, what could be deserving of you could be to follow through things and find the love that exists outside. Yes we sometimes fight to keep the difference that we resemble to the world, the different opinions and point of views that we support with our whole lifestyle, only that in most cases it could fail to reach inside a person's heart.

Only that if you ever breakthrough you're understanding, you can find true love and so much in that path which you traveling. When certainly all the difficulties you've been experiencing in life permanently disappears, and the things that could have refused to give in begins to make sense. From thereon you have find what you needed all along, and if you know the value of it thereof, you keep going through that path and never settle for anything less.

You allow yourself to be ruled by that love you have discovered for someone and everything that you doing. You refuse to be without that tenderness of the heart, you live knowing that you have find something that deeply motivates you from within.

A lot of negative things that we go through happens outside relationships which could've offered us the best in life. Given that regardless of who you are, we all have humble beginnings, where love was true. However, if you ever let go of that kind of a commitment, you will come across difficulties that you didn't know existed, these are some of the issues that will fight you from deep within.

While for a very long time you cannot believe that you are on your own when facing this nature of spiritual battles. You find yourself challenged where only you knows what you doing, is when the integrity of all that you are is questioned, and you don't know how to handle that problem.

You only wish there was some supernatural powers that you can produce to help you pass that terrible situation. Meanwhile you could've tried all that you could, and there's nothing you can do more to help thrive through those difficulties. Maybe if you can choose another path towards your goals things would be better. Only that when your faith has been cultivated within that direction, regardless of what you come across, you cannot go back.

In the path you have chosen about creativity and love, when everything has been taken away from you, and now there's no way you can reach at that level which could allow you to live your dreams. The only route that exists leads to some destruction, where only a few number of people can tolerate as the outcome of their lives. Now you have to fight to keep your beliefs about being a decent human being through that goal which you have discovered in you.

What we are only make sense to ourselves, and no one else outside your world can understand, we all have a certain quality that lives within us. That thing which we have become that we do every time, that makes us unique and who we are, and be grateful that life doesn't make mistakes. It always rewards us for our efforts, and is that which you have been committed to that you will find at the end. Whereas you must live everyday knowing that you can get punished if you do something different which you know is not what you stand for.

When you have thought about everything the way it is, and you know exactly what you want to achieve, goals about your life and relationships. Then nothing can ever go wrong, besides that we at times fail to realize how much we have around us. Only that if you can allow situations to blind you, then you have no one to blame, because regardless of how much we identify ourselves with other people, at the end of the day is your life. You remain alone in whatever you doing, and you have yourself to count on, given that everything will always question you for the intelligence that you resemble.

You must be grateful that the solution to all your problems is what you know, and is that path which you have chosen, which its success will be your new life. That must be enough to help you focus on the route you have begun. Knowing that it has something to offer you in the future, and is for every situation that you struggling with, and there will come a time where you will make peace with the past.

Even when it was in the distant future you hold on tight to it, and remain focused, and confident given that every part of your life will find meaning from its prosperity. Unlike not knowing what you doing, you can lose focus from being in the dark about what tomorrow will bring. You concentrate on the solution as that can help you to shape the coming events in the right direction. That is able to restore your faith in all your plans and goals, until you're able to repair that part which had died in you.

With a good plan in mind confidence can be regained from deep within your soul, and you can build a life that cares about your every need. You might find something worthy at the end, as you not on your own in this path, we are born traveling with our perfect friends and partners. We somehow are destined to meet at the right time, given that you only get to draw human beings closer to you when you've become a magnet.

A lot that we go through are situations meant for us to groom ourselves with, and find an inspiration to be whatever we desire. The path that we traveled to our goals could've different effects on each and every one of us, and bringing it to life could have hurt somewhere so deep that you cannot remember who you are. However, if you can learn to be a discipline human being, you can get to attract the right caliber of people, as you begin to succeed from your acts of creativity. So much died including the love we had as we sought to be content of the future, and mattered to everything that we were, and how we wanted to be happy with our lives, now you must look for a new beginning.

Going forward always remember what you're doing it for, as a lot of what people will resemble, is not the reason why they engage in things. Just that need to have a perfect picture so that you don't find yourself chasing after shadows, forever keep your goals in mind and not to be confused by situations. So that you don't lose your grip along the way when you get to understand that some are doing it for the sake of lies and deceit, and it's unfortunate for you who didn't know much about life.

You brought all that you are, you showed whatever it is that you know to everyone, and "you didn't run out of minor options, you ran out of everything". Then you begin to feel lost, and you start losing confidence in yourself, however, if you can keep in mind what you doing it for. It is so much better given that regardless of what people can do to deceive you, that's what you will find at the end.

A way of life is a spiritual discipline that we must follow through to our heart's desires, love, personal goals, and every form of success that we want to achieve. It is our ground roots and how we are born in this world, and also explains the rules by which we must obey. That is what governs our lives as individuals, and is mostly defined by certain religious beliefs which all humans must adhere to.

It is through this way of life which we are born from, that things begin to make sense. It is the reason why we are this people that we have become. Not only because we traveled through it to the world, it is the only thing which shapes our understanding, the truth that you know which you must follow, is that "way of life".

It is a way of life that redeems our souls from everything that this world can invent or do to us, and to be a success you must find yours and hold on to it. Given that regardless of the fact that it is through it that we've traveled, it is our gateway out of that darkness, or that universe of no hope. So when you chose love as the route that you'll live through, you must work hard to attain that quality of the heart so that you can never be lost again, even when the path is not easy.

Live with pride through it, knowing that you can always count on love to restore your pride and dignity, to guard your soul not to be find wondering about what you intended at the beginning of your journey. Given that an ordinary need you have for life and to be with someone worthy can seek to turn a human being into a miserable thing that everyone will seek to make a fool of. So do not settle for anything less than true love, and go after it with your whole heart keeping in mind that is what will say so much about you.

Love is also a way of life yes, which you must live with confidence in. Only that you need to exercise caution or be fully aware that it is something that can be taken away from you, regardless of how you pride yourself in resembling honesty. As we all have a need for it, and we can't identify ourselves as people who have achieved their goals without anyone loving us wholeheartedly, that's how everyone define themselves in a normal world.

As long as it is still depended on what someone can do for you, then you not there yet, it must be about loving yourself first, and be devoted to it, that will open every door in your life, because whenever you feel lost or something goes wrong, then you just need to look right inside your heart.

True love when you need to have it, seek after it with your whole body, mind, and soul, regardless of what could try to stand in your way, as it leads to some greater path in life, and it doesn't stop where one think it does. It passes all levels of human understanding, and there at the end when you refuse to give up, the love you have in your heart becomes who you are, all lies and deceit end, and it becomes a reality.

One can stop believing in it, when your mind has led your attention to a certain world where people are about their self-centered ideas, and live with no care for what is the most important thing to seek after. How that can belittle the tender you have in your heart, you begin to feel dead inside, however, don't look away, to live, is to love all that we are, our fair share of the human treasure.

Even when the universe has turned into something that makes you feel weak from deep within, if is true love you have inside, remain sure of everything that you doing. Regardless of how you might judge yourself for the person that you have become, that is your only pillar. Given that you can never have an idea of how people have come along, you just know who you are, and how you came about.

As you look at the world of human beings you see yourself and where you standing, and then you realize the harsh lesson from life. That you don't have to be successful now in everything that you doing, until you find love and make it your way so that it can define how far your success must have an impact. It opens our eyes to realize where we are and to reach for the worth in everything that we doing, or you can continue fighting to pass a lot of human beings, and get to that level whereby a lot that you achieve will mean nothing. As you have failed to succeed through true love.

It applies to everything that we want to achieve, even the love that we desire, can have a definite territory, it can be so little that will mean a lot, and all that you need will find meaning from that. You can choose what you are, and how you want to feel about things, and we grew up knowing plenty about creation, and that is without pride, yet it defines the people that we are. If it had no question about faith, we wouldn't mind having so much in a small universe. Only that it questioned the integrity of who we are and what our entire life stands for, and at the end is the whole world or nothing.

Chapter Eighteen

Quality of the Heart

With all the complications that comes with life, a human being begins to undermine the purpose of living for love, or the use of being focused towards your goals. Is how you might feel when looking at the world and what it can throw to you at times. You imagine yourself changing from what you used to, or what you wanted to be, to a level where things can be done with ease.

It seems as if there's no reason to continue in the path that you've chosen, it was in this way of seeking to breakthrough your creativity where loving a person felt like it had no significance. You always have yourself to rely on, everyone out there turns to be unreliable, and relationships being part of who we are that we cannot live without, feels like you can find it where it was once simple.

This way of life towards greater understanding leads to some place, where the truth about who we are becomes difficult to cope with, you fail to understand this new being that you are, and your needs also. Living has always been about people trying to find themselves, where they became lost in the world, or where relationships has cheated, or hurt them severely. Whether you were right or wrong, you try to find some essential truth, or connection to what you use to be, before love left you with nothing to live for.

When all has been taken away from you, questions continue to linger in your thoughts about what you missing. Is it that to seek for knowledge has opened a gap that cannot be closed easily, or by seeking clarity on certain issues you have separated yourself from everything that creates? Now you have to wait until the end when you have found what you searching for, so that you can be part of creation again.

Love hurts so bad, especially when it is affected by so much that has been compromised because of issues that the world has, over what human beings need. When people are side-lined as one seeks to be taken into consideration, and demand to be treated extraordinary with regard to their needs even if is at the expense of others.

Yes we could've been wrong for overlooking our partners at times, yet the real pain comes from having our necessities for life being ignored. When so much isn't going well in our lives, the relationships we have collapses, still, we feel like we had been taken advantage of, and is where everything could have emerged.

People can get hurt, and a lot of things can go wrong, as love touches us somewhere deep inside. Each and every time something bad happens, you want to escape this universe into a world of no hope, trying to kill the good that rules in your heart. As you feel like is that part you have attached to yourself that is weighing you down.

Do we believe in love as we're happy living with someone, or is it that they are reliable and trustworthy? No, we don't stop believing in it, as we have something important to live for, and is through it where we get to share that side of ourselves. We continue with it since we have so much expectation from this world, and that can only be realized from sharing your life with another kind heart. We have a lot to give to each other from that part of our lives, though at times when you're disappointed, it feels like there's no need to keep the person that you are.

Love touches us mostly where we fragile, and when one turns that, into the only thing standing between you and your destiny, it seems as if there's no need to keep going in the direction that you must. When we hold on to our relationships, we don't just do it because it is a simple thing to do, it can become the hardest to cope with, even to carry inside, it might be difficult, and a burden to live with.

Still, it must continue to rule in our hearts, as we are just slaves without it, you can work for so much only that it amounts to nothing. To care for another is the quality of our hearts, and a necessary thing to do, and is that tender of who we are that we must continue to possess in sharing our lives with each other, especially in modern society, and it mustn't be compromised.

To care for our partners becomes the most necessary thing that so many have overlooked, and you never realize how important it is, until you are left with it as the only thing standing on your way to success. When you have fought to achieve whatever it is that you truly desire, you will understand the value of it towards reaching for your independence. As difficult as it could be, you just want to wake up in a world that says you are free to have everything you require, and to love whomever you like.

Regardless of how impossible things could be, you stand there holding your true identity, so to have that quality out of life. Refusing to be part of a world that seeks to change you where you loved truly, as you acknowledge that everything outside doesn't serve your purpose. You refuse to lack faith in your ideas and the fact that, what can bring freedom to you, is what you know.

We have to let these ideas work the way they are, don't change your purpose as you begin to experience this harsh reality, and strive to please the needs of so many out there. Which is part of the people whom you know very well lives to consume others, while your understanding does exist as well, your own will to be whatever you desire.

Do not let pressure turn you into something that you not, change where you must, yet remain holding on to the vision that you have. Transform the world, and with it, live to make an impact, but don't be left behind, be part of your revolution.

You must belong to the idea that you want to see, if you alter your objectives, you compromise the quality of life. Be a genuine visionary, it just takes commitment to your daily routines, and remaining true to who you are, as well as what you need, to achieve greatness in your path. You don't have to know whom to love or how to get there, all that one requires is faith.

However, we still need to stop making commitments when it comes to love only, learn to also commit to your personal goals, which will help improve the quality of your life as well. The chaotic mentality that we man have out there, the extensive drinking of liquor, and the smoking of substances, all requires one to be committed to quit.

That doesn't bring peace within our lives, relationships, and household, love might require one to be much disciplined all the time. Given that this kind of behaviour can have a major impact in achieving happiness, you want to bring joy to your loved ones, and that could be the only thing standing in your way.

Keeping in mind that if you cannot find happiness anywhere, or maybe joy is rather rare to arrive at. Then you need to look no further as you must know that the true pleasure of being alive and content is to be found in the eyes of the ones you have invested your love in.

How can you let anything ruin what you have with the ones you treasure the most, can't you work on improving just a little bit? Fix those areas that needs attention in order to achieve perfection. Why can't you do something that will reflect a positive difference about you? People usually look at what they failed yesterday and think that's who they are, and they can never do it. But why, is it because you could've made a mistake even when your time to commit yourself to change, or success had begun?

We need to let go of the fear that refuses to accept change, there's nothing scary, you will lose a lot, which doesn't deserve your attention or serve any purpose. Yes you will miss so much about your past, yet it is better to let go of your old life, is very sad to actually find love, or what you need at a very late age. How would you think about yourself, you will even learn to tolerate things that are not worthy of who you are.

There's something funny about love or relationships, and you need to ask yourself this question very seriously. As a man or woman, would you rather have your partner taken from you, or better to take someone else's mate? The answer lies within understanding life as an adult, it is not easy to find a person unoccupied, as they're all committed.

It is better to leave your partner, than having him or her cheating on you and go to another relationship, only to learn a life lesson that it is safe to stay true to one person than to cheat. Therefore remaining with the other forever, if this was the transition of love, what is the best thing to do if your lover is having an affair?

As a male, never leave your current relationship, even though you won't love your wife the way you use to, along the way you might meet someone who will appreciate a true commitment. Still, do not stop being with your old lover, remain together, although part of you would have moved on to start a new life. And maybe the same might happen again, however, you could end up finding a path to a good person with a heart so full of caring. As a woman, just stay true to your man, they do lose themselves, but they end up coming back and remaining trustworthy forever.

To you who endured the pain, that's quality of the heart, somewhere someone can give you something very valuable, that's worth living for. For we need to be careful as that could be the exchange of love from one to another, and giving up on what you have could lead to loneliness. You might know so much about life, only that as we grow old the world turns to be very sophisticated, and you could need to save yourself from living alone. So do everything as young as you could to find a good partner, when there's still so much that you both are worthy of, or before you remain with no option, but to take from others.

Live a life worthy of everything you need, and give love with all your heart, and never hold anything back. Regardless of what has happened, if you are a true believer you can never lose hope on finding the right partner to commit to again, because all that you once lived for has disappeared. One of the best qualities of our hearts is to forever remain a loving person, even if is sad, we are never given any option except to understand the need to be true to our essence. Another greater thing that we can do for ourselves, is to treasure each other when so much is still valid, to be early is the only time where relationships are priceless.

As we are never guided on how to do the right thing, and now we have been caught in a very defying situation, and we cannot do anything to help ourselves, when time passes so much changes. So this is as much as you can go through if you still want to remain a human being, given that you never realized early that it is time to commit permanently.

Imagine a life that you can no longer control, and you have no other option, but to fall prey to whatever is available, you have so much to live for, yet you cannot find true love. However, with all that the world can throw on your path, you still are a valid person, why can't we realize that to be committed is a must dignity to have for everyone.

We all can get caught, as we live in a society full of human beings with ambitions, and we have this discrimination among each other as a group of people that we are. You know that in life we only want the same thing, that is regardless of who you are, and there's always a gap that exists, that you must work hard to close for you to have everything realized.

So without realization you can go through a lot of delays in terms of achieving your goals, as you understand that you can never be after something that represents your own needs. No matter what ideas you have, or what organization you represent, you are just being a human that survives on the same thing.

Love is somehow as well, as it is mixed up in all that, and you can't find any comfort, to be happy you must have worked hard to distinguish yourself, or if you are to find someone who is worthy of you. Being in a relationship with a person who has no clear objective of what they're doing, seems more like you're committing a crime, and don't think that the world can stand for that, or let it happen easily.

"When you're not in a marriage, life can somehow resemble something very strange, you find different ideas that exists between two groups of couples when you want to fall in a relationship with someone. The first group doesn't want you to be with anyone even if is just for a day, these are the weakest, they're committed to each other still not married, yet settled in their communion. Once you pass the first day with your mate, you have passed them, they are the gatekeepers of love and relationships.

The second group is family members, married couples deeply committed to each other, and living together every day, they're the second test of love. They don't want you to enter into a serious stage in a relationship, without being truly committed to one another.

They are the everyday challenge in relationships that have doubts to enter into a serious stage, yet insist on being together for the pleasures of the bodies. So they wouldn't let you enjoy what they have without commitment to loving one another, as they have the same thing as well, and it belongs to them. After passing that level you're through to travel the path of love, which can create an understanding that you want to achieve in loving someone".

The pain of living without love can linger in your heart and you just want to change and become a very isolated human being in your respective life. As man and woman we need to realize what we are to one another, that's at the end of the day when you've learned to value someone truly. Given that we are not made to mistreat each other, and use the other to get ahead, we must find the worth in the exchange we have beyond the physical desire that we have today.

If you haven't passed your affairs or that part of yourself you just become too broken to understand what love can do for you. Do not mistreat someone's trustworthiness, don't cheat, cherish each other every day, and if you've truly mastered your understanding, you now know how to avoid heartaches. As you've come to realize how important your partner is.

By understanding how important your partner is, you've just passed everything you needed to know, and your whole journey will be a completely happy one. If you want to avoid all that exist out there, and so much that can happen along the way, find the courage to love more than you did yesterday, don't let your heartbreak too much to ever commit again.

Man can make a mistake of thinking that true love will always be available, and woman can cheat, and you are both heartbroken. So as a male you need to learn how to take relationships very serious from an early age, and the female must always be trustworthy. This kind of behaviour can continue into adulthood if life doesn't stop you from mistreating each other as couples.

Love must be able to accommodate all of you in a way that you are both about the outcome of everything that you doing. Is when a relationship produces complete happiness, and is a blessed communion where you are all happy and is not just for one person, it's about the two of you. Though we can't behave or treat each other in the same way, as you must understand that the role we play is different. However, we care so much for everything that we are to the other and respect one another's differences.

You must be able to find a place in your heart to understand all that is happening, as it is occurring within a relationship that has no power of life. It needs our complete attention, if you don't give it the energy, it might be difficult to deal with the outcome thereof.

So cherish every moment that you get to create good memories with each other, especially the one you love the most. As it has been a very tough journey throughout life, and you should be happy to be together, and rejoice instead of judging one another about whatever could've happened in your lives.

Do not discriminate anyone for what they have become, they've been through their own challenges, and they did fulfill their purpose. Whether they got it right or not, don't put the blame on them that is regardless of how they have turned out, or what the world has come to be. Everyone has traveled their journeys and arrived in places where they wanted to get to, and yes so much that people did could've had an effect on us, yet we can still make our part count.

It doesn't matter if you're on a journey towards achieving your goals, self-discovery, or love, what remains a fact is that you must travel your own way and reach true understanding for yourself. Yes people could be found guilty of changing the shape of reality, but some have not changed a thing, they just improved it. Make it a little bit tough for human beings to have whatever they want before they can have complete clarity, value, and self-worthiness.

Especially if you're not subjected to anything from lack of participation, you could become too much of a threat, as there's nothing that you're bound to. If you want to experience how difficult the world can be at times, try to achieve whatever you desire through your understanding. Then you will get to know that things are not always as easy as we thought of them to be.

What impact can you really make? Remember that in whatever you doing you're playing in the real world, and there's no other platform above the one which you participating at, and if you succeed, you crown the whole universe. Everything that you want is all here, feels like this vast creation is not big enough, to accommodate you as well, with your physical and spiritual needs, and however, you will find your place. And with all that you do, you still need love too, you probably went for more money than ordinary people, so you understand the part where things became changed in value.

The path that we're likely to travel, we owe it to those who have passed, as they're the ones who have created this world from the beginning and made so much that we can respect and honor their lives and hard work. Given that it is where we began our journeys before we could establish our own understanding that made it easy to create a platform for our ambitions. It was through their dedication that we came to understand a lot with ease, and that was able to build a home somewhere deep within us, and maybe sad if you are born in a situation where there are not enough opportunities.

As it does happen that you might be born in a situation where your dreams can be hard to manifest, even if you prayed. Unlike others who found themselves living where there's hope for who they are, and things are possible if you want them to. On that note we were hoping that we could pray for our fellow citizens who have lost faith towards their ambitions as everything could be hard to reach for.

You might need to engage in doing something worthwhile to help spread some love, and as soon as you've done that maybe your path could be easy. If you are capable and with a kind heart you must continuously believe that you can add a positive impact. Most especially if you have had a certain idea realized, and you're confident that a lot can find themselves in that context, or even change the lives of so many around you as well.

That is beside the part where you could've found yourself struggling with reaching for your goals, because yet is not easy to achieve all our ambitions, however, our people need a lot of love too. So if through whatever you've been doing you have had an opportunity to witness success, it would be really great if you can do anything to touch lives.

Even if you can try to look away there's just so much that can affect you in return, and if you don't want to be a subject to whatever exists out there. You need to have done something to show that you are a caring individual, yes it isn't easy to commit part of who you are to other people. Only that if you can dedicate your love and hard work, you could find yourself working towards doing something that resembles that you truly care.

Whatever it is that you can do is better, as long as you doing it with kindness in your heart, can make a big difference. So it could be the doorway to achieving true love, and that's how valuable you could spend most of your time by doing something good. As for ignorance could later have a bad impact on you, or stand in your way when you want to do what you like. You can find yourself being disturbed, or affected by a part of what you ignored, giving a hand has no pride, or any specific purpose to serve, is just meant to achieve happiness at the end.

Do not blindfold yourself saying that you didn't see, while you did, to be ignorant can have a huge drawback later in your life, and that can ruin your plans. Yet to confront things is being good in resembling care, so much can affect you as it could interfere with the love you seek and the way you wanted to be happy loving a person.

Nothing guarantees happiness if you're doing what you like or whatever pleases you, given that you can avoid so much happening around you. Still, at times you can't as everything comes down to the fact that you don't have to obsessively seek to get ahead.

If you didn't know or see is fine, you can look away, still, you might become a subject to situations that are constantly happening around us. So I wanted to find the true love buried deep within me, as it all comes down to that, whereby life can't be a path you traveled without care, we walk with faith and do everything with love.

The End!!!

About The Author

Sibusiso Malvin Tshabangu Born 7 October 1986, South Africa. Founder of Tie publisher and also a writer of a motivational series titled "Stars Do Fall in Love". This is my fourth book which I hope a lot will be able to understand my theme better as it has always been my first and most favorite book as you get to meet me the author and the publisher in person. I could say that this one is very personal and remain my only brand and I hope to take it further from that, given that is what my whole life stands for as a writer, and a publisher. It is my continuation or expansion of my understanding into modernization which emphasizes on the fact that to avoid a lot of what we can define as diseases and medical disorders, man and woman should learn to focus on love, even if you can be a Master in life, on its own knowledge cannot do much, love completes everything that we are.

Other Books By

From The Series Stars Do Fall In Love

1. Individualism

2. Fame

3. The Lady at the Center of my Heart

www.ingramcontent.com/pod-product-compliance
Lightning Source LLC
Chambersburg PA
CBHW051427290426
44109CB00016B/1460